Percolator
JOEY TRUMAN

Whisk(e)y Tit
VT & NYC

Percolator ©2023 By Joey Truman. All Rights Reserved.
ISBN 978-1-952600-37-1
First Whiskey Tit Paperback Edition

Cover And Book Design By Bob Jolly

This is total and complete fiction, even if every word is true. Names, characters, places, and incidents are the product of the author's imagination, and should not be confused with your idea of reality. Resemblance to actual persons, living or dead, events, or locales is coincidental, probably.

Published in the United States by Whisk(e)y Tit: www.whiskeytit.com. If you wish to use or reproduce all or part of this book for any means, please let the author and publisher know. You're pretty much required to, legally.

For Jakers and Anal J, two of the wildest roommates a boy could ask for.

[1]

The screen door was banging against the front door when Buddy woke up. He was already having trouble sleeping. The electricity had been off for two weeks. He was cold. Wrapped up as tight as he could be in the two flimsy synthetic blankets he owned. He was wearing two pairs of socks, long johns and two long sleeved shirts. His head was wrapped in the flimsy blankets as well. He could see his breath. He was upset. Upset with his roommate. With each passing day without heat he was growing more upset. The lack of heat was only part of it. There was no lighting. There was no hot water. The fridge didn't run. No showers, only lukewarm baths that took forever to heat up. The gas was still on. They could still boil water. And they could fry an egg and make coffee. It was cold enough that they could store food outside. However, the raccoons were a constant enemy. Outsmarting them at every turn. Mostly they ate fried eggs or peanut butter and jelly sandwiches. Buddy didn't want to be upset, but his roommate caused this. Caused it in a way that was preventable. But things got out of hand. Now it was too late. They owed the electric company nearly $700. Unless they came up with half of that, they refused to turn the electricity back on. Making matters worse, they were very far behind on rent. Three months behind, in fact. This was at least both of their faults. He couldn't be mad at his roommate for this. The rent was due again. If they didn't pay at least one month's rent, they would be evicted. The notices had been coming for quite some time. The notices now were threatening legal action. Legal action and forcible removal. It was not looking good. As Buddy lay there, his breath coming out in clouds, head wrapped in a nearly useless set of blankets, listening to the screen door whack-whack-whacking against the front door, the wind relentless, cold and worried about what was going to happen next, his roommate started yelling at him from the other bedroom.

"Buuuuudddy! Buuuuuudddy! Go shut the screen, man! I can't sleep!"

Buddy yelled back: "Do it yourself, fucko!"

Guy yelled back: "It's too cold!"

Buddy yelled back: "Whose fault is that?!"

Guy yelled back: "I told you! I mailed 'em! Scout's honor!"

Buddy yelled back: "All nine of them?! Bullshit!"

The roommate's name was Guy. He didn't look like a Guy. He looked like an Augustine or a Bruno. He was short and half-Mexican, half-Italian. His family moved to Casper from Southern California and decided to name him Guy for some reason. Buddy couldn't figure it out. But Buddy very much looked like a Buddy. And as someone that looked like a Buddy, he kind of had the brains of a guy that looked like a Buddy. He did ask once why Guy was named Guy. Guy just shrugged and said: "I don't know, my parents wanted me to fit in I guess." But being a short Mexican/Italian kid named Guy was the opposite of fitting in. Or that is the way that Buddy saw it. He wasn't totally wrong, but he had a very specific view of the world. Mostly because he was an average-brained White kid from Wyoming who was named Buddy and had always looked like he should be named Buddy. Buddy or Fella, or Mister. The kind of person that played in the marching band in high school then went on to work in a hardware store. Buddy wasn't very tall, but he was taller than Guy. He was balding.

Which caused him so much grief that he both shaved his head and wore a baseball cap. He wasn't un-attractive. He looked like he might age well, or possibly the opposite. He looked old for his age. Because of the hair. Guy on the other hand looked like he could still be in high school. He was better looking than Buddy, but he was not very bright in any way. Not that he was stupid. He just had a different way of seeing things. Like taking money from his roommate for nine months to pay the electric bill and then not paying it. Then letting it get so out of hand the electricity got turned off and the money they owed to get it turned back on was too much for either of them to get a hold of. But also, Guy didn't really care. He was the kind of person, had the kind of brain, that couldn't see practical matters in a very clear manner. Owning a checkbook was too confusing to him. The math was too hard. Even though it was just subtracting what you paid from what you had in your account. The concept seemed extremely abstract. So, he just didn't deal with things like that. And Buddy should have known this. Should have never put Guy in charge of the electric bill. But because Buddy was a Buddy, he thought everyone needed to chip in. Even if it meant the electricity would be turned off. Guy really didn't have a clue about it. In his mind he had sent the checks in. He remembered Buddy giving him money all those times. He remembered Buddy harassing him about paying the bills. He just didn't do it. It just never occurred to him to do it. And it is true that he just spent the money. Like it was his own, he didn't do it on purpose. He was genuinely pleased when he would find an extra $45 dollars in his wallet that he didn't know was there. And really, because he was a generous person, he would go out and buy beer or wine or smokes or food for his good friend

Buddy and himself to celebrate the sudden windfall. Which Buddy would relish as much as Guy, and they would have a fine time together eating the food or drinking the wine or beer or smoking the smokes. And really, had Buddy been just a little bit smarter or if Guy had just been a little bit dumber, this never would have happened. The electricity would still be on. Because Buddy would have known better than to give Guy the responsibility of the electric bill and Guy never would have been holding that money in the first place.

Buddy was upset though. He didn't see the truth in the matter. He only saw how Guy was a fuck-up who ruined his life at the moment. The heat was off, and it wouldn't get turned on anytime soon unless they could come up with some money. And rent was due and the money they had together was not enough to pay it. And they owed three months back rent as well. And they were about to get evicted. And it was cold, and Buddy just wanted to sleep. But the screen door continued to whack-whack-whack the front door. The wind was relentless. Because Buddy was so upset, Guy could hear it in his voice when he yelled back at him. He didn't understand why he was so upset, but he could tell he was upset. He was in the same position as Buddy. Wrapped up like a mummy in cheap flimsy blankets. Wearing two pairs of socks, long johns, two long sleeved shirts. Seeing his breath as he breathed. He got out of bed. Ran into the living room. Opened the front door. Fought the wind for control of the screen door. Latched it. Slammed the front door and ran back to his room. Rolling himself up once again in his flimsy cocoon.

He yelled to Buddy: "Happy now?!"

Buddy yelled back: "I'd be happier if we had heat!"

Guy yelled back: "I told you! I paid the things!"

Buddy yelled back: "Liar!"

[2]

The two roommates fell back asleep for a while. The cold air waking them both. Buddy couldn't take it anymore. He got up. He put on jeans and his boots and a denim coat that was two sizes too big for him. He put a stocking cap on. He didn't like wearing it. It made Buddy feel like he looked like a penis. And it made his head itchy. He couldn't wear it to bed for this same reason. Even if it kept his shaved head warm. He would dream about having a penis for a head and then he wouldn't be able to sleep. Plus, it was itchy. At the moment, fresh out of bed, he was willing to wear it though. If only to warm his ears up. When his ears were warm, then he could switch to his baseball cap. He would feel better after that. He walked by Guy's room on the way to the kitchen.

Guy said: "What-cha doing?"

Buddy said: "What do you think I am doing?" He was still upset. His tone came across as extremely annoyed.

Guy said: "Sorry, man, just asking."

Buddy said: "Making coffee, I guess."

Buddy looked at Guy. He was wrapped up the same way he had just been. But he was also using his sheets as an added blanket. That was smart. Buddy looked at Guy's mattress. The number of stains were astonishing.

He said: "Did you make all those stains?"

Guy said: "What stains?"

Buddy said: "The bed stains. That mattress is disgusting."

Guy said: "I don't know. I don't think so. Wasn't this bed here when I moved in?"

Buddy said: "Yeah, right. But still, have you never noticed when you change your sheets?"

Guy said: "Change my sheets? What do you mean?"

Buddy said: "You don't change your sheets?"

Guy said: "I thought you just slept on them until they ripped and then you bought new ones?"

Buddy said: "Hasn't anyone complained?"

Guy said: "Who's going to complain?"

Buddy said: "You had the one girl here that one time."

Guy said: "Oh, I don't know. I don't remember us talking about sheets. All I remember is the lettuce."

Buddy said: "Oh, right, the lettuce. Haha. She was wild. How come you never called her?"

Guy said: "I did. She said she moved."

Buddy said: "Oh, right, but wait! Where did you call her at?"

Guy said: "I don't know, her house I guess."

Buddy said: "But she had moved?"

Guy said: "I don't know, man! Why the million questions?"

Buddy said: "I think she was fucking with you, man."

Guy said: "Yeah, I don't know. What the hell do I know about moving? Maybe she said she would call me back or something. What the hell do you care about it?"

Buddy said: "Hey! I am just curious is all."

Guy said: "No, you are not. You are just trying to make me feel bad like you always do."

Buddy said: "C'mon! That's not true. Seriously! I was just curious. She seemed nice."

Guy said: "Bullshit! She wasn't nice at all. She wanted anal sex. Then I found that lettuce on my dick and then she told me she moved. Leave me alone! I'm tired."

Buddy smiled, remembering the night. It was a good memory.

Buddy said: "You want an egg?"

Guy said: "Yeah, I guess."

Buddy said: "Hey, don't be mad, it was a funny night is all."

Guy said: "Well, don't rub it in."

Buddy said: "I'm not rubbing it in!"

Guy said: "Well, it didn't work out, now leave me alone about it."

Buddy said: "Yeah, okay. You fucked her in the butt and got lettuce on your dick, though. It's kinda funny."

Guy said: "It's not as funny as you think it is."

Buddy said: "It's pretty funny."

Guy said: "Yeah, I know it's funny, but don't rub it in okay?"

Buddy said: "Yeah, I know, sorry."

Guy said: "Yeah, okay."

Buddy said: "Yeah, well, you want lettuce with your eggs?" Guy got out of bed at this point and ran towards Buddy. Trying to tackle him before he got away. Buddy got to the kitchen and turned around. Guy had run into the wall and had given up chasing him. He had an erection poking out from his long johns. Buddy saw it. He laughed and said: "Dude! That was totally turning you on! Lettuce-Boy! Still thinking about dropping it into that chocolate lettuce starfish?" Guy looked down. He was indeed erect. He pulled his long johns down and waved his erection up and down at Buddy.

Guy said: "Yeah? You wanna suck it?"

Buddy said: "Jesus Christ, man! Put that thing away!"

Guy said: "You asked for it! Have a taste, fucker!"

Buddy turned around. He went into the kitchen. Guy got dressed. He wanted to shut his bedroom door and whack off to the memory of the girl with the lettuce butthole. But he knew that Buddy would know what he was doing. So, he didn't do it. He put jeans on. A parka and a stocking cap. Guy didn't sleep with his stocking cap on either. For the same reason that Buddy didn't. Because it was too itchy. But unlike Buddy, Guy had a full and thick head of black hair. His ears got cold though. So, he wore the stocking cap during the day. He also had some wool mittens that folded over and turned into fingerless gloves. He pulled those out of his parka pockets and put them on. Folding the mitten parts back. Connecting the Velcro attachments to themselves. Guy went into the bathroom and unbuttoned his jeans and pulled his semi-erect penis from his long johns. It took a while before his penis deflated enough to go to the bathroom. He finished and flushed. Putting his things back. He could hear eggs frying in the kitchen. Guy was suddenly very hungry.

[3]

Guy went into the kitchen to watch Buddy fry the eggs. There was a coffee percolator on the stovetop. It was an odd contraption that Guy had found in a box down the street quite a while ago. Neither of them knew what it was called or how to use it. They both assumed it was for making coffee. It was a clear glass carafe with a lid and an insert that was a tube with a tuna can-like cup on top that had holes in it. There was also a lid for that part. That also had holes in it. They both thought it looked cool, but because they didn't know how to use it, they left it on the counter. Collecting dust. Then the power went out, and suddenly there was no way to make coffee. The drip coffee maker was electric. Naturally. The way they figured out how to make coffee in the percolator was quite clever for these two. They correctly understood that the coffee grounds went into the top part with the tube. They correctly understood that the water needed to boil. But they couldn't quite grasp that they could fill the carafe with water up to the line it suggested you fill the water to. Then put the tubed part with the tuna can with holes into the carafe. Then put the coffee grounds into the tuna can with holes. Then put the lid with holes on that. Then put the final lid on. That lid had a glass hat in the middle of it. Which confused them the most. What they did to figure the thing out was they decided the water needed to boil, so they filled the carafe to the line it said to fill it to. While that was happening, they put coffee grounds into the tuna can with holes, then put the lid with holes on top of the coffee grounds. They discovered that they couldn't grab the tube anymore when they did this, so they took the lid with holes back off. They waited for the water to boil. When it came to a boil, Guy—because Buddy was too afraid the thing would blow up, or burn him somehow—pinched the top of the tube and lowered the tuna can with holes attached to the tube into the boiling water. This did burn Guy's hand. Because the water shot up the tube and into his palm. Buddy was standing next to him with his hand on the burner, just in case he had to turn it off because of an emergency. And that is exactly what he did. He turned the gas off. The water stopped shooting out. Guy yelped and ran to the sink to run cold water over his palm. Buddy thought for a second. If the water comes out when boiling and doesn't come out when not boiling, therefore a lesser boil will make less water come out. He was not wrong. He turned the burner back on, immediately turned the knob to the lowest point and waited. At first there was nothing. He increased the heat a little bit. Still nothing. He increased a little more. Suddenly a little spout of water came spurting out. Then another. Then the water drained down the coffee grounds and the water started turning color. They both were amazed. They couldn't believe this science. They felt like geniuses all of the sudden. They high fived, which made Guy yelp again because of his burned palm. Then they stood there watching the thing percolate.

Guy said: "How do we know when it's done?"

Buddy said: "I don't know."

Guy said: "What about these other two parts?"

Buddy said: "I don't know."

They watched the water turn a darker and darker brown. Then it turned black. Buddy looked at Guy, Guy looked back at Buddy. He shrugged. Buddy turned the gas off. Then he said: "Oh! Now I get it! You put the holed lid on top of the grounds, so they don't fall out when you pour the stuff out, and then the top lid holds everything else in!" He put the holed lid on top of the tuna can with holes. Then he put the main lid on. Guy grabbed two coffee mugs. Set them on the counter next to the stove. Buddy poured out two steaming cups of hot coffee. The look in their eyes was one of pure joy and self-satisfaction. Like they had just solved the Grand Unified Theory in Physics. For sure somebody was going to come over and give them a prize for geniusness.

But it was quite clever for them. They had worked together to solve a problem. Not only that, but they went on to improve their solution to the percolator. A thing they called the "Bubbler." The next time they made coffee Buddy heated the water to boiling. Guy filled the tuna can with holes with coffee grounds. He had a pair of tongs on hand to pinch the top of the tube. Buddy turned the gas off when the water started to boil. Guy lowered the tuna can with holes and tube down into the freshly boiled water. Then Buddy slowly brought the water back up until the Bubbler started percolating. After that they both stood there staring. Waiting for the water to turn black. Then Guy would get two mugs and put them next to the stove and Buddy would put the holed lid on top of the tuna can with holes. Then he would put the main lid on. Then he would pour two cups of steaming hot coffee into the mugs. It was a thing of beauty. A foolish thing of beauty, but a thing of beauty, nonetheless.

Buddy and Guy did this beautiful routine when the water started to boil. The eggs had been fried and were waiting on plates. When the beautiful Bubbler routine was finished, they stood there in the kitchen. Guy in his parka, Buddy in his denim coat. Both wearing stocking caps. Guy with his foldable mittens. Eating their fried eggs. With salt and pepper. Drinking their coffee. Black. Guy couldn't drink milk. It made his guts hurt. And Buddy was suspicious of milk for reasons that were not entirely clear. Back before the electricity went out, Buddy would often buy a quart of milk and eat cereal with it. But then halfway through the jug, he would declare that it was not good anymore and dump the rest down the drain. Guy didn't care. If he drank milk, he would shit his pants. The mystery went unsolved. However, like everything with Buddy, there was a direct correlation between him declaring that the milk had gone bad and something that happened in his life before this point. But because Guy couldn't drink milk, he wasn't interested enough to find out why Buddy was so wishy-washy with his milk. A phrase that Guy used all the time when describing the actions of his friend, Buddy. Buddy was very wishy-washy. He had plenty of things that he did that didn't make any sense to anyone else but himself. Like the eggs. He liked them over-easy. Like Guy. But if there wasn't a little bit of hard yolk in the middle he wouldn't eat them. He would declare them to be poisoned. Dump the eggs in the trash and fry two more. Guy hated when he did this. He would have gladly eaten the eggs. And because of Buddy's cooking technique, he could never tell if they were done to his satisfaction until the eggs were on the plate and he was eating them.

He would say to Guy: "I wouldn't eat those if I was you."
Guy would say: "They're fine. Delicious even."
Buddy would say: "Your funeral." Then fry up two more eggs.

The eggs they were eating now passed muster with Buddy. He finished the eggs and licked the plate. Put it in the sink. Guy did the same thing. Guy always did this. Licked the plate when he was done. A thing that Buddy thought was very gross. But now that they didn't have hot water, it was easier to clean the plates if they licked them when they were done. At first, he found the practice embarrassing. Even shameful. But after a couple weeks, he didn't notice anymore. He actually enjoyed it. The last little lick of yolk and salt and pepper was kind of a nice way to end the meal. They stood there drinking coffee. The cups steaming profusely in the cold air. The wind blowing outside. They were miserable, but also somehow happy. Buddy was feeling bad for being angry at Guy about the electric bills. Even if he hadn't actually said anything about it. Or done any of the violent things he thought he might do. He felt guilty and had to come clean.

Buddy said: "Man, I know that you didn't mean to do it, but we need to figure out this heating thing, like now. I don't know how much more I can take. It's the end of

March, man. Are you sure you can't call your parents or something? Just borrow a few bucks?"

Guy said: "Nah, man, I told you, my mom said if I came around again, she would call the cops."

Buddy said: "Well, what about your sister?"

Guy said: "What about your sister?"

Buddy said: "I guess I could call my dad, but he has less money than we do. Fuck."

Guy said: "What about your mom? Didn't she say she saved all that money for you to go to college?"

Buddy said: "Well, she did, but she said it because she thought I would go to college, I don't think she was offering it to me."

Guy said: "Yeah, but she has it."

Buddy said: "I think you are missing the point, man. She ain't as bad as your parents, like, I mean, she won't call the cops or nothing if I go over there, but she won't give me any money, I can tell you that. She'll tell me to ask my dad and then spend twenty minutes telling me about how much of a deadbeat he is. How he owes her back money. From like child support stuff."

Guy said: "Well, what if I went and asked her? I met her that one time, she liked me. Maybe I could offer like a trade-off or something?" Guy was seriously asking Buddy if he should go ask Buddy's mom to exchange money for sex.

Buddy said: "Are you serious?"

Guy said: "I'm just sayin."

Buddy said: "You think if you go ask my mom to pay you for sex for our electric bill she will say yes? Is that what you are saying?"

Guy said: "I don't know! I just thought we were thinking about things!"

Buddy said: "Dude! You are out of your fucking mind! You want me to go ask your mom if she wants to bone me for the electric bills? I can pull a piece of lettuce out of her for you."

Guy said: "Oh, come on!"

Buddy said: "What?!"

Guy said: "Well, first of all, she would pinch your fucking dick off, and it would be as easy as a bird biting a worm, the tiny thing you got going, and then my dad would put you in the grave."

Buddy said: "Whatever, mine is bigger than yours. You just showed me that tiny thing you got flapping. Or at least I thought that is what I saw, sadly my telescope is at the mechanic so we may never know."

Guy said: "Oh, yeah?! Whip it out and let's see!" Guy meant it. He was going to take his penis out and compare it with Buddy's.

Buddy said: "Okay, relax. Your dick is just fine. We need to figure this shit out though. Another month of this, or who knows, I mean, it's not even April. How much money do you have?"

Guy said: "I got half the rent or something."

Buddy said: "Yeah, right. Me too. I don't know. Go get your money. I'll get mine."

Buddy and Guy went to their rooms. Each one grabbed their money but left a little behind. Both of them getting their money from under their mattresses. Both of them looking over their shoulder when they left the other money behind. Both of them knowing exactly where they both hid their money. It was a farce, in a sense, they were not lying to each other, but neither of them wanted to be without money, just in case something came up. Guy returned to the kitchen first. Then Buddy. He waited until he could hear Guy leaving his room before he left his own room. He was afraid that Guy would sneak in and get the extra money and claim it as his own. Guy didn't have this thought. His relationship with money was so unconventional that it didn't occur to him that Buddy was kind of a snake. Not that Buddy was actively going to steal his money, but that Buddy had a different relationship with money that Guy did not have. And yes, Buddy would steal Guy's money at any time, telling himself that he earned it because Guy had stolen all that electricity money, and therefore he deserved it, but Guy, Guy would only steal Buddy's money if he needed it for something. Like a hotdog, or some smokes. And then he would forget all about it. And Buddy would ask him where he got the money for the smokes or the hotdog and Guy would truly have no clue. Saying something like: "I don't know, I found it on the ground or something." Then Buddy would go check his stash and know that Guy had stolen from him, but he would say nothing. Just fume. Which created a very odd feed-back loop about things and finance between these two. That Guy would never steal from Buddy, but Buddy would easily steal from Guy, but Guy wouldn't even know he was stealing from Buddy, but Buddy knew he was stealing from Guy, but only Buddy would feel bad about it, which would make him upset, but he was powerless to bring it up, but at the same time Guy was constantly stealing from Buddy, but because he didn't realize he was doing it, he was innocent. And clueless. And impossible to pin down.

They put their money on the counter. Buddy counted it twice.

He said: "We got rent. Almost exactly. We have to pay it. We just have to."

Guy said: "Yeah, alright. I guess. I'm sick of eating eggs and peanut butter, man."

Buddy said: "Would you rather sleep in the gutter?"

Guy said: "No."

Buddy said: "Well, we have to pay this. If we don't, we are screwed."

Guy said: "Okay, you going to pay it now?"

Buddy said: "What do you mean?"

Guy said: "I don't know. Are you going to go pay this now? I don't like that it is all stacked up together. How much did you pay?"

Buddy said: "For rent?"

Guy said: "Well, no. But, I mean, yeah, kind of. Didn't I put more on my part than you put on your part?"

Buddy said: "Dude! You got the heat turned off! And now you are worried about a few twenty dollars?!"

Guy said: "Well, it's kind of a big difference, isn't it?"

Buddy said: "For rent or the electric bill?"

Guy said: "Well, what does the electric bill have to do with anything?"

Buddy said: "You're what? What?! What does the electric bill have to do with things? Are you serious?! I gave you like four hundred dollars that you just pissed away! What do you mean?"

Guy said: "But that's not rent, right?" Buddy wanted to start screaming at Guy, but his passive-aggressive nature made him shut down.

Buddy said: "Fine! Let's go down to the place together and get a money order. You can watch me put the thing in the mailbox."

Guy said: "Yeah, okay. That's cool." Guy's relationship to money was coming to terms with Buddy's relationship to money. And they still had no plan on how to deal with the electric bill.

Buddy said: "Well, let's do it now, then."

Guy said: "You sure they'll be open?"

Buddy said: "Well, it's mid-morning. I don't see why not."

Guy said: "But it's windy, man."

Buddy said: "It's always windy!"

Guy said: "Yeah, but do I have to go?"

Buddy said: "No! You don't! But you just accused me of not, what the fuck, man?"

Guy said: "I just don't understand why you are paying less rent than I am is all."

Buddy said: "I'm not!"

Guy said: "Yes you are! You put less money in the rent pile, how is that not less rent?"

Buddy said: "Because you didn't pay the electric bill! You owe me hundreds of dollars!"

Guy said: "Not for rent, I don't."

Buddy said: "It's all the same! The rent, the bills, they are all the same thing!"

Guy said: "Nuh-huh, when the rent doesn't get paid they don't turn your room off or something."

Buddy said: "Yes, they will! If we don't pay this month's rent they will very much turn the apartment off. A cop will come around and throw us out of this place!

Guy said: "But can't we just tell them what is up?"

Buddy said: "You have a brain like a porch-swing! Why am I even arguing with you?!"

Guy said: "I deserve to know where my money is going."

Buddy said: "Come with me, we can pay the rent together. You'll have a real lesson to learn, it might expand your idiot brain!"

Guy said: "I just don't understand what the rent and the bills have to do with each other. How can we be living here but also be so cold? I just don't get it."

Buddy said: "I don't know. I don't like it either. It's fucking freezing and they cut the heat off, what can you do about it? All I know is that they will kick us to the curb if we don't pay the rent. If that happens, we are fucked. I mean, we are already pretty fucked, but without a place to live, it's gonna suck. So, yeah, I don't know."

Guy said: "But it's so windy."

Buddy said: "Yeah, it's always fucking windy."

[4]

Buddy went into the bathroom. Guy sat down on the couch. Waiting. He got cold so he stood up again. He went into the kitchen thinking he would drink more coffee. He instead just stared at the percolator. He was vexed by the thing. Confounded. Flummoxed. Baffled. What a strange and complicated device. As hard as he tried to understand it, he just couldn't. How did the water get up the tube? Who would design such a thing? Why were there so many steps? The drip coffee thing made total sense. You pour the water in the back, then you put coffee grounds in the top. You turned it on and coffee came out. But the lids and the tubes and the tuna can with holes, the tongs and the pre-boiling of the water? He stood there staring until Buddy came into the kitchen.

He said: "Ready?"

Guy said: "I gotta go to the bathroom." Guy stayed staring at the percolator. Buddy became impatient.

Buddy said: "Well?"

Guy said: "Well, what?"

Buddy said: "Don't you have to go to the bathroom?"

Guy said: "Yeah?"

Buddy said: "What's the hold up? You glue your shoes to the floor or something?"

Guy said: "No, why would I do that?"

Buddy said: "Cause you're not moving!" Guy turned around and started lifting his feet up and down off of the linoleum.

Guy said: "See."

Buddy said: "No, you idiot, why aren't you going to the bathroom?"

Guy said: "I am waiting."

Buddy said: "For what? The turtle to bite a hole in your underwear?"

Guy said: "No, what?"

Buddy said: "What are you waiting for?!"

Guy said: "Oh, Jesus, just ask a question if you are asking a question, no need to get mad at me."

Buddy said: "I'm not mad at you, you're either dense as hell or you're fucking with me, why, Guy, are-you-waiting-to-use-the-bathroom? Yo comprehende?"

Guy said: "I am waiting for your stink to leave. Why else would I be waiting?"

Buddy said: "See! You are fucking with me!"

Guy said: "I'm not! Scout's honor! You went into the bathroom and took a shit, now I am waiting for your stink to leave so I can go in there and take a shit. Are you happy? Did I spell it out good enough for ya? Jesus!"

Buddy said: "I guess, you could have just said that."

Guy said: "I did."

Buddy said: "No, you didn't."

Guy said: "Nuh-huh! I said, I am waiting for the stink to leave and you said, what are there gumballs under your shoes and I said, no, and then I proved it and then you yelled at me." Buddy couldn't take this conversation anymore so he switched the subject. He said: "Why were you staring at the Bubbler?"

Guy said: "I don't know, I just can't understand it. How does it work?"

Buddy didn't know, but he was the kind of person that thought that he knew and walked around confidently explaining things he didn't understand to anyone that would listen. Half of the time he had an inkling that he was unsure, but once he started talking, he would convince himself that he knew what was going on. In the end he would become convinced that he was correct and would argue to the death against anyone that disagreed with his conclusions. This tiny detail of Buddy's personality was the largest reason that he and Guy were such close friends. Most people in society found this kind of specious reasoning and out-right non-truths annoying to argue about, but also quite irritating and obnoxious. Not Guy. Guy took everything Buddy said literally and absorbed it. Buddy was the smartest person he knew. He could talk about anything. Make sense of anything. And then explain it in a way that Guy could understand. Guy had no clue that Buddy was less than righteous. Less than forthright. Less than correct. Had he known, well, who knows, the idea that Buddy was a charlatan was something that never-ever crossed Guy's mind. And because it never-ever crossed his mind, Buddy took advantage of that. This didn't mean that Buddy was manipulating Guy, probably the opposite. Buddy didn't know he was a charlatan. In his mind he was also the smartest person Guy knew. He was certainly the smartest person he knew. Meaning, Buddy. Meaning, himself. Because Guy would listen to his meandering and specious reasoning and eat it up, suck it down, chew it with gusto, and then declare Buddy a genius because it felt good to Buddy. It also felt good to Guy. They were simpatico. Buddy was slightly older, he had been around longer than Guy, he had a lot to teach the poor dum-dum, as Buddy liked to refer to Guy. Not in a disparaging way, but with love and a sense of protection. As much as Guy was mostly a confused and almost beautiful butterfly floating around in the breeze, Buddy was like a tiny bird, a tiny bird that thought he was an eagle, soaring to great heights, showing Guy the world from his clouds-height view, but really he was just a small thing, a sparrow, at best, too small to eat butterflies, but slightly faster and more obnoxious than a butterfly. Bouncing from limb to limb, making tons of noise. Flying off into the distance when the smallest infraction happened near him. They were meant for each other. And it was a thing worth admiring. They wouldn't win any awards with their brain power, but they were friends to the core. Deeper almost than brothers. Because neither of them had brothers. A thing that made their lives very lonely before they ever met each other. They both had sisters. However, both of their sisters were much older than they were. Growing up alone and without brothers had made both of them crave something that they didn't know they were craving. And when they found each other, it was truly a thing worth admiring. Something that all the smarts in the world could not provide them with. It was admirable and ineffable, and it was a thing. A very big thing. An instant love that transcended time. And society. It was deep and noble. And from a distance it was quite a thing to behold. But like children playing alone in a room without adults, when you looked closer, if you looked closer, if you listened, you were both filled with love in your heart, because these two were so very sincere with each other, and at the same time, listening to their conversations was an exercise in bemusement. Like hearing one child say to another child: "He had to go to the hospital because he swallowed chewing gum and it got stuck to his heart." And then the other child saying: "I got gum stuck in my hair once and my mom had to use clippers. I wonder what kind of gum it was?" And the other child saying: "Probably some really sticky gum, like the kind I'm not allowed to have anymore. You wanna go play pirates?"

Buddy looked at the percolator, thought about it for a second. Wondering where he should start. He had no clue how the thing worked. He would figure it out on the way.

He said: "Well, you got to start with cold water, I have noticed that cold water is the best water, it sits well in a glass, unlike hot water, which is trying to move away from the edges, which is how steam works, steam is like a, um, ladder that the water molecules climb up the edge of the glass and then jump off into the air. Remember that. You got a pen and paper? You will probably need to write this down."

Guy looked around. There was no pen and paper.

Buddy said: "I'm just joking."
Guy said: "Oh."
Buddy continued: "So the best way to get the water flowing is to start with cold water in the glass part. That way the glass can hold onto the water on the bottom and keep it from crawling up the sides of the glass thing, which it is going to do when it gets hot. And you have to remember that the tube in the middle is metal, so it behaves different than the glass because the glass is trying

to stay like hard and the metal is trying to bend and shrink, right?"

Guy said: "Yeah, right. Because metal is bendier than glass. That makes sense."

Buddy said: "Right. So, in order for the water molecules to not climb up the side of the glass thing you have to keep the metal tube thing cold, which is why it is connected to the tuna can thing, because the coffee grounds need to hold the thing down so the water molecules can't climb up the side of the glass, which is why the tube thing tapers out like that on the bottom. The roundy bottom of the tube is basically a mouth for hot water molecules which would normally crawl up the side of the glass thing, but because the tubes are metal and there are coffee grounds weighing the thing down, the hot water molecules have nowhere to go, and because there is three things happening, the metal from the tubes, the glass from the glass thing, and the hot water molecules, everything gets confused and the hot water molecules are looking for a way to climb up the glass walls, but they find it easier to climb up the metal tubes, and then, because the coffee is weighing everything down, the hot water molecules climb up the tubes, spurt out onto the coffee grounds, and then they want to get hot again, so they go down to the bottom and climb up again. It's simple human nature, man. The easy way out is the best way out. And that's it. Hot coffee."

Guy said: "Whoa, man, that's deep. Do you think the water molecules have brains or what? How do they even know what to do?"

Buddy said: "It's simple, they aren't so different than you or me, man, like, touch a hot stove, you know what I mean? You don't want to burn your hand. You burned your hand, remember that?"

Guy said: "Yeah, it sucked."

Buddy said: "Yeah, imagine if you had like a million hands! All burned at the same time! I'm surprised this thing doesn't just explode. My guess, my guess! Is that if we accidentally put the top lid on when the thing was boiling, we would get blasted by glass. It would be like a bomb in here! We would both lose an eye and even worse! It wouldn't surprise me if the whole apartment blew up! Cut us both in half. The police would be picking up chunks of our bodies off of an airplane flying by."

Guy said: "Whoa."

Buddy said: "Yeah, right?"

Guy said: "Um, maybe we should switch to tea? I didn't realize we were putting ourselves in such dangerous ways, ya know?"

Buddy said: "Nah, we're fine. Just as long as the lid isn't on when the water is boiling, we'll be fine."

Guy said: "Okay, good." Guy looked like he was about to smash the percolator on the kitchen's linoleum. To keep the good friends safe. Buddy noticed.

Buddy said: "You're that worried, huh?"

Guy said: "I wasn't, until you said what you just said."

Buddy said: "Just keep the top lid off and we'll be fine is all. Where are you going? Don't be upset." Guy had turned around from looking at the percolator and was leaving the kitchen.

Guy said: "I can't wait anymore."

Buddy laughed. He had left the bathroom in a pretty horrible state. He opened the window and the wind was blowing like crazy. Maybe it had sucked the stink out. Guy would have to live with whatever was left there inside. Buddy looked at the percolator after Guy left. He wondered if anything he had just said was true. He didn't know. Now he was convinced that the thing would blow up if they left the top lid on when the thing was boiling. It was a very odd feedback loop. There was no point of reference. Since Guy never pushed back when Buddy went on specious pedanticism like this, Buddy was left feeling both confused and vindicated. Forcing himself to believe his own nonsense. He now thought, without a doubt, that if they left the top lid on the percolator, the Bubbler as they called it, it would blow the entire city block to smithereens, so much so that he, Buddy, was now as worried about the thing as Guy was. Buddy heard Guy yell: "Damn, dog! What did you eat!" as he went into the bathroom. Buddy chuckled. He could hear the wind blowing against the building. He was cold and wished the heat was still on. Buddy put his hands in his denim coat and stared at the percolator. Wondering how it actually worked.

[5]

Buddy stood there looking, listening to the wind. He had forgotten all about the percolator soon after Guy had left for the bathroom. He lost focus the second he tried to remember what he knew about boiling water. His thoughts went straight to science class in high school. Which reminded him of high school. Going to high school. Being in high school. And that was it. High school was the last thing he wanted to think about. Things were supposed to be different. He wasn't supposed to be standing in a freezing apartment with the electricity cut off wondering how to pay rent and bills. He wasn't supposed to be in Casper. The wind caught his attention. He felt angry again. Not at Guy this time, but at everything. Especially the wind. The relentless wind. It was unbelievable, the wind. It just never stopped. It only increased. There were days when it would nearly stop for a few hours. Days when suddenly everyone was confused about what was happening. Why the pressure had changed. The endless needling from the mountains. People would find themselves unable to walk correctly. Without the constant pushing against them, the resistance, they would find themselves stumbling down the sidewalk, bumping into each other. Having to hold onto things, like fences and parked cars. Unsure if something was wrong. And without the endless whoosh in their ears everything sounded different. Louder, clearer. Like a hangover had descended from the heavens and affected all living things with sensitivity and a mild nausea. The nausea came from their bodies trying to correct for the sudden change of motion. They were all suddenly hungover, standing on a boat, or so it felt.

The confusion would lead to some wild mood swings. The constant wind gave the people of Casper a sense of constant struggle, constant adversary, so much so that when that thing went away, they didn't know what to do about it. Half of them became paranoid that something was wrong, and danger was lurking in all directions, the other half suddenly felt like everything was finally okay with the world. They would start to make plans, begin new projects, maybe call old lovers and see if they wanted to go for another round of things. A sense of optimism would descend on half the population. While the other half became darker by the minute. Certain the end was coming. That at any moment a stranger would approach from somewhere unseen and stab them, or the phone would ring and a dear loved one would be dead. And these two different kinds of people would find themselves meeting in places, like restaurants, or gas stations, or work. Things would be tense. There would be tension. On one hand it was hard to see others so happy when you were so miserable, on the other hand, it was hard to see people miserable when you were so happy. And those that were happy would want to help those that were unhappy become happy. And those that were unhappy would wish misery on those that were happy. In the end they would reach some sort of middle ground where everyone was neither happy nor unhappy, just on edge wondering how the world had suddenly gone crazy. And then, just as easily and quickly the wind had died down, it would start up again. At that point the entire town of Casper, Wyoming would let out a sigh of relief. Balance would be restored. Everyone would go back to normal, feeling slightly embarrassed at what had just transpired.

Percolator

Guy came into the kitchen and looked at Buddy, who was looking at the percolator and listening to the wind.

He said: "What are you doing?"

Buddy said: "What do you mean?"

Guy said: "You're just standing there."

Buddy said: "Yeah."

Guy said: "Are you depressed or something?"

Buddy said: "I don't know, it's windy."

Guy said: "It's always windy."

Buddy said: "It's really windy now." Guy listened to the wind. It was quite windy.

Guy said: "Yeah, it is really windy. Good point."

Buddy said: "Don't you get sick of it?"

Guy said: "The wind?"

Buddy said: "No, being an idiot. Yes, the wind!"

Guy said: "Why are you always so mean to me? What do I know about what you are talking about when you are just standing there looking like a horse or something. I can't read your mind, man."

Buddy said: "Yeah, I'm sorry, I didn't mean it. Casper, man, it is a real bummer-town picnic. Maybe we should just move? We don't owe these jerks shit. We got the rent money. Maybe we could move to Denver or something? I bet it's less windy there. Plus, they got stuff happening and what not."

Guy said: "You think? Whoa, are you serious?"

Buddy said: "I don't know, a thought, I guess. Why not?"

Guy said: "Well, we don't really have a car."

Buddy said: "We could take the bus."

Guy said: "Or really know anyone in Denver."

Buddy said: "We gotta know a few people, I think that one dude from that thing a few weeks ago said he was moving to Denver."

Guy said: "Yeah, I guess, but so what? It's not like he will let us crash at his pad and stuff, how would we even get in touch?"

Buddy said: "Why are you being so negative, man? Normally you are Mr. Positive."

Guy said: "I know, I'm just worried. Denver is big and scary, and we don't have any money."

Buddy said: "We have to know somebody with money! Right? Someone can help us out. Think!"

Guy said: "Well, we could work more. I think we are going to have to get out of this mess we are in."

Buddy said: "Yeah, I guess, but I would rather borrow money from somebody and pay them back when we get some sweet jobs in the city, wouldn't that be better? If we work more, we will be here forever, I don't want to be here forever. I am sick of being here now. Listen to that. It sounds like it's going to rip the siding off. I can't take it anymore!"

Guy said: "I mean, we could sell our stuff?" Buddy laughed at this. He looked around.

Buddy said: "What do we have? A couch, an ancient television, a couple beds and a Bubbler? Maybe we could hock our towels and that gross nudie mag you found in the dumpster?"

Guy said: "Hey, that thing is golden. You've borrowed it a few times, I know it."

Buddy said: "Like hell!"

Guy said: "Either that, or you been rooting around my room when I'm not here."

This was true. Buddy rooted around in Guy's room when he wasn't there, and Guy rooted around in Buddy's room when he wasn't there. This was something that Guy would admit to, but Buddy, on the other hand, would not admit to. So, he lied.

Buddy said: "Yeah, you got me! I did a wank or two with those buxom ladies. I couldn't help it! I had run out of memories to keep the juices flowing."

Buddy looked at Guy. Waiting for him to accept the lie. Guy accepted the lie.

Guy said: "I knew it! I thought I was crazy thinking I had put the thing one place and then it was somewhere different, you dirty dog, see?! It helps. You think you are so cool sometimes, but I got you this time, you like the same things I like, you just can't admit it!"

Guy was triumphant. Buddy let him have his moment of victory. At the same time thinking about all the times he had violated Guy's personal space.

Buddy said: "You got me! I'm sorry! I just couldn't help it. A man's got needs, you know."

Guy said: "All is forgiven. All you have to do is ask. I'll lend you the thing, man."

Buddy said: "Yeah, I should have…"

Just then the screen door broke loose and started banging against the building. Buddy sighed and went over to latch it again. When he opened the front door, the wind blew it into the apartment. Buddy's stocking cap blew off. The wind was cold and fierce. Like a blast of tiny, iced teeth. Or iced sand. Or a sheet of freezing glass. Buddy struggled with the screen door and latched it again. He shut the front door. Bent down and picked up his stocking cap. His bald head was cold because of the wind. His hands were cold too. Buddy put the stocking cap on. Pulled it over his ears. He put his hands in his denim jacket. Went back into the kitchen.

Guy said: "Pretty windy out there."

Buddy said: "It is."

Guy said: "Should we go pay the rent, or what?"

Buddy said: "I don't know. It's kind of windy."

Guy said: "Wait for it to die down then?"

Buddy said: "Yeah, prolly."

Guy said: "Yeah."

Buddy said: "Yeah."

Guy said: "I'm bored."

Buddy said: "Me too."

Guy said: "We could smoke."

Buddy said: "We got no cigarettes."

Guy said: "Right. Wait, but I thought we had some left?"

Buddy said: "We did, but you insisted we smoke them all last night, remember? You had some theory about how you would find a pack on the ground today because you were feeling lucky?"

Guy said: "Oh, right. Maybe that is why I feel so greasy today? I forgot. We could get drunk?"

Buddy said: "We drank all the beer last night as well, remember? You said it wouldn't matter, tomorrow was your lucky day."

Guy said: "Right! No, I don't remember that."

Buddy said: "Well, that is what you said, and for some dumb reason I went along with you. Now we got no smokes and no beer."

Guy said: "Why didn't you stop me?"

Buddy said: "I don't know, you were so convinced, who was I to say 'no' to you?"

Guy said: "Yeah, but we would be better off right now. What was I thinking?"

Buddy said: "I don't know, you had a plan."

Guy said: "Well, that sucks."

Buddy said: "It does kind of suck."

Guy said: "We could play cards, I guess?"

Buddy said: "Yeah, I guess."

Guy said: "What? You don't want to do something? We gotta do something!"

Buddy said: "Well, I would almost rather get back in bed, at least that way I would be warm."

Guy said: "And then what? Stare at the ceiling?"

Buddy said: "I don't know, maybe take a nap or something, I didn't sleep so good last night. I was too cold."

Guy said: "C'mon! A nice game of cards, we could get the Bubbler going again, it'll be fun! I swear!"

Buddy said: "What, here in the kitchen? My hands are freezing, and you got those nice mitten things. I don't know."

Guy said: "Put your hands in your pockets, I'll go get the cards."

Buddy said: "What about the Bubbler?"

Guy said: "Take the lids back off and heat the thing up again! C'mon! Let's have some fun times!"

Buddy took the lids off of the percolator. He ignited the burner. He kept a close eye on it as Guy went into his room to find cards. Buddy was convinced the thing would explode at any second. Sending them both into the ether. The wind blowing against the side of the building. The smell of coffee in the kitchen. Buddy put his hands next to the burner. Trying to warm his fingers up. Unsure if he was seconds from death. He was thrilled and scared at the same time. Part of him wanted to be done with it all, and the bigger part, the more realistic part, wanted to go back to bed and get warm and maybe take a nap. Buddy was exhausted. The wind, and the rent, and the electricity bill, and the future. Guy, even. Buddy felt a certain loyalty to Guy, but he was feeling so exhausted with reality that he didn't know what to do about it. Guy was a butterfly to his eagle, a puppy to his mastiff, a tiny worm to his robin, he couldn't abandon him, but Buddy was not feeling very good about the future. He didn't want to let on that he was feeling this way. At the same time, he had convinced himself that the percolator, the Bubbler as they had defined it, would blow up at any second and send them into oblivion. Buddy watched the percolator with great intent. Waiting for Guy to get back.

[6]

Guy came back with cards. He put them on the counter. Face down. The top card had a picture of a man straddling a chair sideways to the camera, he was squatting, his erect penis thrusting through the back of the chair.

Buddy said: "Whoa! What are those?"

Guy said: "Cards."

Buddy said: "I can see that, but what is that on the backs?" He picked up the cards. Rifling through them. The cards were pornographic. All males. All singular men. Erect in different poses. They were pornographic, but there was something innocent about the photographs. Almost vulnerable. The men seemed like they were enjoying the photo session. Genuinely pleased to be posing naked. Very comfortable in their vulnerability. The pictures were almost un-sexual. If you were to cover up the bodies, from the neck down, you wouldn't have guessed at the nature of the photographs. They would merely be a stack of handsome young lads having a lark for a photo shoot.

Guy said: "They're all I got."

Buddy said: "Where the hell did you find these? Whoa! Look at this guy!" The man on the card was standing naked, erect, next to a ten-speed bicycle.

Guy said: "Let me see!" He looked. "You can't ride a bike naked, that'd be insane."

Buddy said: "Where did you say you found these?"

Guy said: "I thought I showed you these before? I must have. I found them on the sidewalk. I could have sworn you were with me. Who else would have been there?"

Buddy said: "I feel like I would remember that. Were we drunk?"

Guy said: "I don't know, probably. I think we were coming back from the bar or something. I don't know. I don't remember either."

Buddy said: "Well, shit. They are something else. Who the hell would buy these things? And where the hell would you get them?"

Guy said: "I don't know, maybe from the back of a nudie mag or something? Isn't there that shop out on the Outer Drive? The one for adults."

Buddy said: "Yeah, maybe. Weird. And how do you just lose them on the sidewalk? How does that happen? You're just walking down the sidewalk one day with your porno cards and happen to lose them on the way to your card game?"

Guy said: "Yeah, I don't know."

Buddy said: "Weird."

The coffee started percolating again. Buddy shut the flame off. He dumped the dregs from their coffee mugs into the sink and filled them back up again. He looked at the mugs. The pictures on the side. They were also pornographic. Buddy had known this. Had been looking at them for months. Ever since Guy had brought them home. Claiming he had found them on the sidewalk. The pictures on the mugs were of very buxom ladies in classy poses. Buddy remembered Guy bringing them home. They both had a big laugh about it. Why anyone would be throwing them away neither of them could understand. The mugs were too fantastic to be trash. Buddy was starting to see a pattern in the things that Guy was finding on the street. A thing started percolating in his brain that he didn't know how to articulate just yet. But he was finding it odd that Guy had a propensity for finding these things seemingly randomly on the street. He had some questions, but he wasn't sure what those questions were. He blew steam from his mug and took a sip. He looked into Guy's big brown dumb eyes and wondered what he was thinking. He was taking a sip himself. A woman with huge breasts was smiling at him while he did this.

> Guy put the mug down and said: "Okay, what is it? Five Card Stud? Go Fish? Rummy? Slapjack?"
> Buddy said: "Dealer's choice."
> Guy said: "War it is."

He dealt the cards. One to each until the deck was empty. The idea was simple. The highest card won. That person took the two cards. Put them in his deck. Then they kept going. The one who ended up with all the cards won. The cards were face down when you played them. Flipping from the top of the stack. Aces were high. Guy flipped a six over. Buddy flipped a nine.

> Guy said: "Damn."

Buddy took the cards. Guy flipped a queen over. Buddy flipped a seven.

> Buddy said: "Damn."

Guy took the cards. This went on.

Buddy said: "Damn."
Guy said: "Damn."
Buddy said: "Fuck."
Guy said: "Ah, yeah."
Buddy said: "You know it!"
Guy said: "Shit."
Buddy said: "Damn."
Guy said: "Damn."
Buddy said: "Fuck!"
Guy said: "In yo' face!"
Buddy said: "Fuck."
Guy said: "Play a real card, sucker!"
Buddy said: "Fuck."
Guy said: "Hot streak, coming through!"
Buddy said: "Loser!"
Guy said: "Takes one to know one!"
Buddy said: "What the?"
Guy said: "Damn."
Buddy said: "Damn."
Guy said: "Damn."
Buddy said: "Damn."
Guy said: "Damn."
Buddy said: "Damn."
Guy said: "Damn."
Buddy said: "Damn."
Guy said: "Damn."

Percolator

>Buddy said: "Damn."
>Guy said: "Damn.
>Buddy said: "Damn."
>Guy said: "Damn."

This went on until the decks were finished. They gathered their winning cards and started again. The game was pure luck. A time killer. But there was something about it that reflected the mood of the morning. The luck of being poor and unable to pay the rent. The electricity being turned off. The wind too intense to deal with. That, combined with the mere luck of the draw. The temporary good feeling of winning, followed shortly with the shame of a temporary defeat. That no matter how many cards you stacked on your side, you were going to lose them because of random chance later in the game. You couldn't hold on to the good ones and play them strategically. You could only play the one unforeseen one you had at that moment. And if it was good, good for you, and bad for them. But if it was bad, well, bad for you and good for them. The game went on and on. The wind blowing. The nudie mugs steaming hot coffee from a mysterious percolator. All of it both random and tragic, but not random or tragic. They could have played a different game. They could have gone out to pay the rent. They could have done anything, really, but they didn't. They chose to stand there, burning time and saying: "Damn." Neither upset nor un-upset with the results. As long as they had cards remaining, they were still in the game. And it wasn't so much a reflection of their circumstances as it was a reminder that there was nothing really that they could do to change things. Sure, they could go pay rent. But then what? They wouldn't have any money left. Aside from the very small amounts of cash that both Guy and Buddy had kept hidden in their secret places. The one secret that they held from each other. A secret that Buddy was aware of and Guy was aware of. Which wasn't actually a secret at all. But if they paid the rent, they would be totally broke. The electricity was cut off. Buddy was depressed and he couldn't admit it. Guy was probably depressed, but because he had a personality like a dog, he took things as they came, much like this game of War, a thing that, Buddy, as much as he would refuse to admit it, admired about Guy, because Guy didn't really think about things, and Buddy did, and Buddy, who by all measures was not dumb, was not smart enough to understand that he and Guy were almost the exact same person, but Buddy refused to admit defeat, and Guy, a person who did not accept defeat, who just rolled with things, but was too, well, a little to the side of personal reflection, Buddy did not see himself as somebody like Guy, just rolling down the road, finding porno stuff on the ground wherever he put his feet, no, Buddy was a man of his own making, he would not admit defeat, even when he was outgunned, outnumbered, out of cards, no, Buddy would still fight, even if the fight was useless and dumb and broke his heart and made him feel like a loser. Buddy respected Guy for his ability to just roll with things. To meet things at their own level. To constantly be playing a game of War with his life. Because, what? In the end, what did it matter? You lose some, you win some. You would either say: "Damn." Or you would say: "Suck on that, loser." But in the end as long as you had another card to play, you were doing alright.

And the game went on. It kept going on. At a certain point the game was mostly a 50/50 game of chance. Until a moment came along when the odds in your favor diminished with each hand you played. When you had mostly high cards and very low cards. But the number of cards you had left to play decreased with every loss. And then all your high cards had been replaced by average cards that couldn't withstand the onslaught of almost exceptional cards. When you couldn't beat a nine, because all you had was sevens and below. And then. Then when you were down to your last three cards. It didn't matter if you had a seven or a three. Eventually your cards would go from three to two to one. And the last card that you played. Even if it was a seven. Wouldn't beat an ace. It wouldn't beat a king. It wouldn't beat a jack, or a ten or a nine or even an eight. You could match with a seven, but then you wouldn't even have an extra card to challenge. And you would be out. Done. And War, exactly like life, was a game of attrition. You found yourself bereft. With nothing. And on the other side, they had everything. The wind still blowing. The lights still off. The apartment cold as the elements. A notice of eviction waiting to be opened. Slid under the door. Not posted, like the usual mail. And it was then. Then, when it finally occurs to you that it is all over. That there is no coming back from this resounding defeat. This is when you can finally give up and bid farewell to this thing we call living. This is the place where all things go to die. But there is hope in death. Because what is waiting on the other side is just as real as what this life is. And as long as there is hope, there is still something else to be grateful for, and that thing is the simple possibility of change. Change is the harbinger of life. The opposite of death. And even if one can see the stack of cards scraping the skies upon us, nearly toppling from the weight of riches and disgusting greed, with no structure to keep it secure, there is still an option. And that option is to get out of the way when the building topples over. To be a rat outside of the crashing building is much better than being a rat on the inside. And it is better to be an alive rat than a dead rat.

[7]

The card games didn't last very long. War was too random and purely a game of chance. They switched to Poker. A game Guy was incredibly terrible at. Buddy enjoyed winning at first, but he soon figured out that Guy didn't understand the game and therefore was exactly zero competition. This made winning fun-less. They switched to Blackjack, but without any stakes the game was only slightly more fun than War. Buddy got an idea that they should use the rent money to bet with. He split it into two piles. Giving Guy one pile and holding on to the other pile. This helped. They played quite a few hands. Buddy winning most of them. Guy was too optimistic about his chances and tended to go over. Meaning he went above the winning number, which was twenty-one. Meaning he would take too many cards. Meaning he was about as bad at Blackjack as he was at Poker. Buddy lost interest. Guy didn't lose interest, not because he found the games interesting, but because he didn't really understand them. For him the games were difficult and intriguing. He wasn't enjoying losing, so he didn't mind too much when Buddy put a stop to it all. They stood there looking at the pile of money and the nudie cards on the counter. Buddy had his hands in his denim coat pockets. Guy folded his mittens over his fingers. Buddy was jealous of these gloves.

He said: "Man, where did you get those? I wish I had a pair."

Guy said: "Oh, I don't know. I think my mom gave them to me for my birthday or something. Here, take 'em. I can just put my hands in my pockets." Guy started to take the mittens off.

Buddy said: "No, man! I'm fine, I just like them is all. Why do you always got to do that shit? You make me feel terrible."

Guy said: "Do what shit? I didn't do nothing."

Buddy said: "You're always giving me stuff and junk. Stuff you need, stuff you like. It's weird. You're too nice. I mean, I would never do that to you, you know?"

Guy said: "You wouldn't give me your gloves if I needed them?" He was kind of hurt by this admission from Buddy, his best buddy in the world.

Buddy said: "No! You dum-dum, that's the thing, I don't need them. I just like them, is all. It doesn't mean you should give them to me, you're like a goddamned dog that way. You need to learn to stand up for yourself."

Guy said: "But you really wouldn't give me your gloves if I needed them?"

Buddy said: "No, of course I would! If you needed them, I would give you whatever the hell you wanted! Here, you want my coat?"

Buddy started taking off his coat. He expected Guy to say no. Guy did something Buddy didn't expect. He waited for Buddy to take off the coat. He took it from him and put it on. Then he took off the mittens and handed them to Buddy.

Guy said: "There we go. A nice trade. You're right, I didn't need your coat, but since I got it, I don't need the mittens anymore."

He put his hands in the denim coat.

He said: "Ooh, the pockets are even warm."

Buddy put the mittens on. They were nice, but now his upper body was cold. He couldn't figure out where Guy was going with this odd thing he had just done. He decided to call his bluff and keep going with it.

Buddy said: "Well, alright. A nice trade indeed. These gloves are fantastic!"

Guy said: "Mittens."

Buddy said: "Mittens now, but if I do this…"

Buddy folded the mitten part back.

"…now they are gloves."

Guy nodded like Buddy had just done a magic trick.

Guy said: "Wow! You're a regular Houdini!"

Buddy looked into Guy's big brown empty eyes. Was he just fucking with him? What the hell was going on?

Buddy said: "Are you fucking with me, man? What the hell is going on?"

Guy said: "No, man, those mitten/glove things are cool, where did you get them?"

Buddy said: "From you, you jackass!"

Guy said: "Oh, right."

Buddy said: "Okay! I give! You win! Give me my damn coat back, I'm freezing."

Guy took the coat off and handed it to Buddy. Buddy put it on. He didn't take the mittens off. He pulled the mitten part back on one of them in order to zip the coat up. He flipped the mitten part back over his fingers. Guy put his hands in his parka pockets. Buddy was unaware that he was now wearing the mittens. He knew he was wearing them, but he was unaware that he should give them back to Guy to complete the trade-back. This was what Guy had planned to have happen. He knew it would happen this way. He had tricked Buddy into taking the gloves and Buddy was unaware of it. Guy knew Buddy very well. He was easy to manipulate. Mostly because he was incredibly selfish, but also because he was incredibly arrogant. In his mind all things that were good that happened happened because Buddy had planned them. And all things bad that happened happened because someone else was at fault. And Guy, who was not the brightest amongst the living people in Casper, was aware of one thing, you could get Buddy to do almost anything if you could convince him it was his own idea. And Guy, who was a good person, who only wanted the best for his friend, Buddy, wanted him to have the mittens. And in a stroke of virtuosic empathy and tenderness had just convinced his good friend, Buddy, to take the mittens from him even though he didn't need them. This act of friendship held these two together. Buddy was insanely selfish. Petty even. He had no friends aside from Guy. Not because he was incapable of making friends. Buddy was charismatic, charming even. He could make friends very easily. But keeping friends was a different thing altogether. Most people got sick of him pretty fast. Buddy was aware of this and it hurt his feelings. He tried to hide it, his disappointment, but Guy had seen it. Too many times. So many times that it hurt Guy's feelings to see Buddy getting rejected. So Guy made a promise to himself to protect Buddy from these bad feelings. To be a true friend to Buddy. Even when he was abusive. Or bullying. Or plain mean. Which was a thing that looked good from a distance, but in practice, the longer these two knew each other, the more their relationship took on some sort of dependency issue. Where Buddy needed Guy to keep him from feeling bad about himself and Guy needed Buddy to act like the big brother he had never had. Their relationship was not exactly healthy, but it wasn't unhealthy either. It bordered on toxic at moments. Especially when Buddy was feeling the worst about himself. When he made Guy feel like garbage just to make himself feel better, but those things, those times, Guy had no problem speaking up, yelling back, defending himself. So, when Buddy would say things like: "Guy, you need to learn to stick up for yourself," Guy knew this was a moment when he should do something nice for Buddy in order to change the mindset of his best friend in the whole world. Who was not feeling too good about himself at that moment. And this was a thing that Buddy interpreted as Guy being weak. Being too magnanimous. And, yes, maybe Buddy didn't need the mittens, he wanted them though. He even said as much.

That he was jealous. And Guy, a person that did not really care about material things, he had no problem giving his best friend in the whole world his mittens. And so, it was easy to trick Buddy into taking the mittens. He felt bad that Guy was so nice and he, Buddy, was actually an asshole, which made Guy feel bad for Buddy, so as simple as that understanding was, all Guy had to do to get Buddy to take the mittens was to force him to act like a decent person for one second and then, when Buddy wasn't looking, because he was distracted by benevolence, he could transfer the mittens to Buddy's hands and the magic trick was complete. Because Buddy was not benevolent by nature. He was blinded by his own niceness. Doing his best mental tricks to make it seem like it was him, Buddy, who had done all the good things in the world. When in fact it was actually Guy who did the good thing.

So, yes, in a sense, Guy was like a dog. If being like a dog meant that you did things without really thinking about them. And, yes, Guy didn't think this tradeoff through, like how you would go from point A to point B. First, I ask him to trade the coat for the mittens, then I give him the mittens, then I give him the coat back and voila! He has the mittens. Guy, however, was virtuosic like a dog. He instinctively knew what Buddy needed, even if Buddy wouldn't admit it himself. Like bringing a newspaper to him while he sat in his reading chair smoking his pipe. It wasn't a sinister thing that Guy did. Or even a thing of exchange. A thing of material realities. It was something easy and simple. There was nothing cynical about it. Guy wanted his good buddy to have the mittens. Buddy wanted the mittens but was too proud to ask for them. All Guy did was simply give Buddy the mittens and by doing so, Buddy was convinced he had made the whole thing happen on his own. With his own thoughts and ideas. That Guy was a dum-dum who would give his last dollar to a hungover millionaire who just needed a Taco Tuesday while lying in the gutter next to the drive-through. And Guy was okay with Buddy thinking that. Because Guy understood that Buddy wished he could do that same thing. And as much as Buddy was an eagle to Guy's wimpy worm drying on the hot sidewalk after a rainstorm had passed, Guy was the moral compass that Buddy had never had in his life. And it made him want to be a better person just by being around the guy.

And, yes, they did have a toxic relationship, because Buddy was quite abusive, emotionally, but Guy had a thick layer of defense around himself. He was no stranger to abuse. He was Mexican in Casper. Mexican in Casper with a name like Guy. A name his parents thrust onto him because they thought it would help him fit in. But had done the opposite. He had never fit in. Not in middle school or high school. He was always an outsider. A Mexican with a generic White name. In a very White community. Guy spent nearly all of middle school and high school known as "El Guy," or "Guy Taco," or "Mexican Guy." And there was nothing he could do about it. He tried to complain to his parents at some point, but they told him to toughen up and to just embrace it. To "act more White." And Guy tried to act more White. But it changed nothing. He was always going to be the "Spic," or the "Wetback," and so it was. He was bad at school anyway, so it didn't really matter. School was just something he needed to get through. In a way, he and Buddy were similar in this way. Buddy didn't have to deal with racism, but his personality kind of isolated him the way that Guy's name and heritage isolated Guy. Which was a thing that Buddy would never understand, but Guy, being the empathetic person he was, he was able to connect with Buddy for this reason. And Guy, even after all the years of abuse in school and his parents lacking sympathy for him and Society being pure garbage at all times, he never lost his inner core. His openness and willingness to be a good person. So, yes, he and Buddy had a toxic relationship. Mostly because Buddy was not the best of friends, he said things to Guy that were awful and hateful and unwarranted, and Guy did everything in his power to make Buddy's life good and pleasant and liveable, Guy was not beaten down by Buddy's abuse. He knew exactly who Buddy was. Deep down, Buddy was scared and alone. Guy knew that Buddy was not racist. He couldn't give two shits about what Guy was. Where Buddy's abuse came from was based on what Buddy thought of himself. And because Guy had been subjected to so many abuses over the years, Buddy's assaults were not so much a critique of who Guy was, but more of a reflection of who Buddy was and what he wanted to become. Guy didn't see Buddy calling him a "dum-dum" as an indictment of Guy, he saw it as Buddy calling himself an idiot for not being a better human being. And this thing alone, whether it meant they had a toxic relationship or not, whether Guy should simply punch Buddy's lights out at all times, it didn't matter, because Guy didn't care, and Buddy didn't mean it.

And, yes, both Guy and Buddy depended on each other, they were both isolated and needed each other because of it. And the truth of the matter, the real truth of the matter, if Guy wanted to, he could take Buddy down in a single fell swoop, a carefully worded response to Buddy's abuse could destroy the guy. In a way that Buddy would not be able to recover from. He was living on the edge of something very precarious, and Guy knew it. And because Guy had spent his life battling this same abuse, he was better equipped to deal with it. Buddy, on the other hand, he was weak and sensitive and fragile. And it is true that Guy saw Buddy as a big brother to him, he also knew that Buddy was so tender, so freaked out and worried about every single thing in the world, that Guy couldn't help himself when it came to Buddy's insecurities. He had no problem giving the guy his mittens. Because it meant that Buddy would stop thinking about the mittens and maybe start explaining the percolator again. So Guy could finally understand how it worked. Because, as much as Guy was an emotional genius, he was actually a dimwitted moron when it came to cards and things of science. Like a percolator. And as much as Buddy was a science genius, he was the absolute worst when it came to emotions.

They stood there in the kitchen. Cold from the heat being turned off. The electricity. Buddy wearing the mittens. Guy with his hands in his parka pockets. The rent money on the counter. The perverted cards stacked up.

Guy said: "What now?"
Buddy said: "I don't know."
Guy said: "Drink more coffee?"
Buddy said: "Nah, my stomach hurts."
Guy said: "Should we go pay the rent?"
Buddy said: "The wind is pretty bad, we should give it a second."

Guy said: "Yeah, I guess. Maybe I'll go lay down. I'm kind of tired of standing up."

Buddy said: "Yeah, I guess."

Guy said: "Alright then."

Buddy said: "Yup."

Guy walked out of the kitchen. Went into his room. He untied his boots and kicked them off. He got under the covers. Lying on his back. Looking at the ceiling. The weird drywall work that looked like dripping mud. The singular sconce, looking like a boob in the middle of the ceiling. With no light coming out of it. The room was cold. Dry. The wind blowing outside. The window shaking. Buddy did the exact same thing. Except his room didn't have a window that was shaking. His room was darker than Guy's. But the door was open, so the light came in. Buddy looked at his ceiling. His sconce was just as boob-like. The shadows of the dripping mud were more depressing than Guy's dripping mud shadows. Buddy didn't know there was a difference. But there was. A difference. Buddy thought he had the better room. It was bigger, for sure, but it didn't have any natural light. Which wouldn't matter, except the power was turned off. So, Buddy's room was now darker than Guy's room. Buddy was glad that he was wearing the mittens. He was a little confused as to why he had them on. But he was glad that they were on his hands. He was happy to be in bed. For the first time in hours, he was more warm than he was cold. Buddy started to think about things. Which was something he liked to do. Guy, however, thought about nothing. He went straight to sleep.

[8]

Buddy woke up scratching his head. The stocking cap making it itchy. The screen door was again whack-whack-whacking against the building.

He yelled: "Guuuuuy! Guuuuuy! Go shut the screen door!"

This woke Guy up. The wind was rattling his windows. The wind was screaming. Whistling. Guy scratched his head. His stocking cap was making his head itch.

"Guuuuuy! Did you hear me?!"

Guy yelled back: "You heard it first! It's your turn!"

Buddy yelled back: "I did it last time!"

Guy yelled back: "But it's cold!"

Buddy yelled back: "C'mon, man! Be a pal!"

Guy got out of bed. He ran to the front door. The door flung open when he turned the knob. His stocking cap blew off. He went onto the porch and pulled the screen door closed. It took all the strength he had to do this. He pushed the front door closed. As he was bending down to get his stocking cap the screen door sprung open again. Guy turned the front door knob. The door flew open. This time it made a hole in the wall where the knob hit the sheetrock. Guy wrestled with the screen again. He managed to get it latched. He pushed the front door closed. Bent down to get his stocking cap. The screen door sprung open again. This time he didn't try to shut it. He looked at the hole in the wall the knob had made. Went back to his room and got back into bed.

Buddy yelled: "What happened?! Why didn't you shut the screen door?!"

Guy yelled back: "I did! Twice!"

Buddy yelled back: "But it's still whacking the building?!"

Guy yelled back: "I know!"

Buddy got out of bed and went to the front door. He yelled: "What happened to the wall?!"

Guy yelled back: "The door flew open!"

Buddy yelled back: "My ass! What did you..."

He was opening the front door when it flew open, slamming into the wall. The knob going into the hole it had made. Buddy went onto the porch. His stocking cap blew off his head and into the living room. He struggled with the screen door. Using all his might. He managed to latch it. He pushed the front door closed. He bent down to get his stocking cap. The screen door unlatched and started whacking against the side of the building. Buddy sighed. He gave up. He went back to his room and got into bed. He felt a sudden and overwhelming amount of frustration. He was on the verge of tears. He couldn't believe what was happening. Everything felt ashambled. He didn't know what to do. Where to turn. Who to turn to. His mom wouldn't help him. His dad couldn't help him. Guy would try to help him, but that wasn't any help at all. His sisters wouldn't help him. Guy's parents wouldn't help either. Nor his sister. He got back out of bed and went into Guy's room. Guy had his wimpy blankets down below his crotch and was furiously masturbating. Buddy cleared his throat. Guy opened his eyes and turned to his side. His naked butt aimed at Buddy.

Guy covered himself and said: "Dammit, dude! Ever hear of knocking?"

Buddy said: "The door was open."

Guy said: "You could still knock!"

Buddy said: "Knock-knock."

Guy said: "Real cute."

Buddy said: "Man, we really need to figure this shit out. I can't live like this."

The screen door whack-whack-whacking against the building was louder in Guy's room than in Buddy's room. The wind was louder too. Screaming and whistling. The noises somehow made the room feel colder as well.

Buddy said: "Are you sure you can't ask your mom to borrow some money?"

Guy said: "I already owe her a ton of money."

Buddy said: "Well, maybe we can move into the apartment above the garage? At least that way we would have heat."

Guy said: "They rent it to a college student. Plus, we already tried that before. Remember? She said, 'No way in hell.' Remember?"

Buddy said: "Oh, right. But that was a while ago. Maybe she changed her mind?"

Guy said: "That was like three months ago, I don't think anything has changed since then. I mean, I don't even think I could get my old room back at this point."

Buddy said: "You'd just move out on me like that?"

Guy said: "Oh, no, never! I just mean she is pretty pissed at me right about now."

Buddy said: "What did you do?"

Guy said: "I told you, I owe her a bunch of money."

Buddy said: "But that's old hat."

Guy said: "Not really." Buddy stood there rubbing his stocking cap around his head. Scratching the itching. His hands still in mittens.

Buddy said: "How long?"

Guy said: "I don't know, a couple months?"

Buddy said: "What did you borrow it for?"

Guy said: "Rent."

Buddy said: "Well, you didn't give it to me."

Guy said: "Would you have used it for rent?"

Buddy said: "Well, prolly not, but still."

Guy said: "Well, what's the point in paying the rent if it doesn't get paid?"

Buddy said: "Well, you could have held onto it at least. Then we could at least pay the electricity bill."

Guy said: "Well, hindsight is like fifty/fifty, man."

Buddy said: "Twenty/twenty."

Guy said: "What's twenty/twenty?"

Buddy said: "Hindsight."

Guy said: "Really? I thought it was fifty/fifty, like flipping a coin. You know? Win some, lose some?"

Buddy said: "No, you dum-dum, it's like a vision test thing. Twenty/twenty means you have good eyes."

Guy said: "Well, that doesn't make any sense. Why would you have good eyesight in the future and not now? Do you get glasses or something?" Buddy sighed. He wanted to stay focused, and Guy wasn't making it easy.

Buddy said: "But what did you spend the money on?"

Guy said: "I don't know, stuff I guess."

Buddy said: "Anything of value? Something we could sell?"

Guy said: "We drank all the beer, smoked all the cigarettes, ate all the Taco John's. I mean, I bought a couple cool shirts."

Buddy said: "Yeah, okay. Fuck, I mean, we have to do something."

Guy said: "Why don't we just pay the electricity bill with the rent money and then figure out the rent money?"

Buddy said: "If we don't pay any rent then they are going to kick us out of here. I told you that."

Guy said: "I know! That doesn't make any sense, though."

Buddy said: "To you or to them?"

Guy said: "Both!"

Buddy said: "Man, I don't make the rules. I mean, you aren't wrong, we could pay the electricity and be warm until they evict us. Which isn't the worst idea, but I don't know how soon that would be if we don't pay the rent. Like maybe they would come with cops in a couple days and all that money we give to the electric company would be wasted."

Guy said: "Or maybe not. Maybe they take a while to come kick us out and in the meantime, we somehow make some good money?"

Buddy said: "Like how?"

Guy said: "We could take extra shifts and stuff."

Buddy said: "Are you out of your mind?"

Guy said: "What?"

Buddy said: "Did you really forget that we were fired?"

Guy said: "Fuck, right!"

Buddy said: "Do you smoke pot or something? Is that what you spent the money on?"

Guy said: "No, man, I just forgot! Jeez! We were only working two shifts a week as it was, sorry for living."

Buddy said: "You're like a goldfish, man. How do you even remember to put socks on in the morning?"

Guy said: "I sleep in my socks."

Buddy said: "You're missing my point."

Guy said: "I get your point. I am an idiot. Thanks for being a dick."

Buddy said: "Sorry, it's just nuts you can't remember that."

Guy said: "I remember! I just forgot is all."

Buddy said: "Well, it won't help us now. We should probably go pay the rent. That will buy us some time."

Guy said: "But it's so windy."

Buddy said: "But we got to do it. It needs to happen."

Guy said: "The cops won't come around in this wind, only insane people are out there fighting this shit."

Buddy said: "I think everyone is out there fighting this shit. It's just you and me stuck inside with no heat and no rent. Most people have jobs, you know?"

Guy said: "Really? You really think that the town is dealing with this shit? Listen to that. That screen door is about to blow off the hinges."

Buddy said: "Yeah, really. People have lives, Guy. It sucks, but they do things. They don't just sit around all day whacking off because the wind is too much."

Guy said: "Yeah, but the door bonked a hole in the wall, that seems pretty intense."

Buddy said: "Well, I mean, you go to work and it isn't windy inside and all. We used to do it when we had jobs, right?"

Guy said: "Yeah, sure, I guess. But still, I don't feel like going outside."

Buddy said: "Me neither. But we should probably go pay the rent. Just in case."

Guy said: "Yeah, but what if the money blows out of your pocket? That would be a tragedy."

Buddy said: "That's insane. Don't be insane."

Guy said: "You never know, man. Anything is possible."

Buddy said: "The money won't be sucked out of my pocket."

Guy said: "You don't know that."

Buddy said: "You just don't want to go out into the wind, man."

Guy said: "Neither do you."

Buddy said: "But I am willing to risk it, we need to pay the rent."

Guy said: "Can't we just do it tomorrow?"

Percolator

Buddy said: "I suppose, but it will just be as windy tomorrow."

Guy said: "You don't know that. Tomorrow might be all birds chirping and sunshine."

Buddy said: "The sun is shining now. It's just a little wind, man. C'mon! It'll be a blast! We can get some beer and smokes on the way back. Take a break from being miserable."

Guy said: "But we don't have any extra money."

Buddy said: "Right." Buddy had a thought. "Well, what if we make the rent out for less than the amount and then buy some beer and cigarettes with the extra money?"

Guy said: "Well, why not pay the electricity bill and then send the other money to the landlord with a note that says we will pay the rest soon?"

Buddy said: "I don't think it works that way. But maybe. Maybe you are onto something. What if we went and talked to the electric company and begged them to turn the heat back on for like half of what we owe them and then send the rest to the landlord and make a note that says the rest is in the mail?"

Guy said: "Would they do that?"

Buddy said: "I don't know, I have never tried."

Guy said: "But what about the beer and cigarettes?"

Buddy said: "I mean, we could just take that off the top, nobody would know the difference."

The two roommates felt like they were planning a bank heist. Like they were pulling the wool over somebody's eyes. Even though they were merely deferring funds they did not have. Buddy was convinced this was a great idea. Rent would kind of get paid and the heat would get turned back on. Once the heat got turned back on, they could maybe think straight. And then, when they were thinking straight, they could figure out some things. Plus, they could celebrate with some beer and smokes.

Guy said: "Well, alright then. Let's get a move on." Guy wrestled around under the flimsy covers to pull his pants up. He stood up. His back to Buddy. Buddy turned around and went into the kitchen. Guy followed him. Putting his hands in his parka pockets. Guy said: "Well?"

Buddy said: "I don't know, man, it is windy as shit."

Guy said: "Yeah, but we need to barrel through, right? Isn't that what you said?"

Buddy said: "I never said that."

Guy said: "You said something like that."

Buddy said: "I think I changed my mind."

Guy said: "C'mon, man! Are you serious?"

Buddy said: "I don't know, I mean, I'm already cold, and it's windy! What's the rush?"

Guy said: "Fuck that! C'mon! You take the money." Buddy grabbed the money and put it in his front pocket.

Guy said: "You sure it's secure?"

Buddy said: "You think I'm an idiot?"

Guy said: "No, but."

Buddy said: "Don't worry about it."

Guy went to the front door. Buddy followed him. Guy turned the knob. The door blew open. Slammed against the sheet rock. The knob going into the hole the door had made before. Guy pushed the front door back into place. Guy said: "Yeah, alright, you may be correct." Guy followed Buddy back into the kitchen. They stood there looking at each other. The perverted cards.

Guy said: "Well, what now?"
Buddy said: "I'm hungry."
Guy said: "Same."

[9]

Buddy said: "Eggs or peanut butter and jelly?"
Guy said: "I don't know, neither?"
Buddy said: "We could make egg sandwiches."
Guy said: "That sounds gross."
Buddy said: "I could fry up some peanut butter?"
Guy said: "Are you serious?"
Buddy said: "No, I'm not fucking serious, bone-brain."
Guy said: "Well, no reason to be a dick about it."
Buddy said: "Well, you know damn well we only got eggs or peanut butter and jelly, unless you got something special hidden in that damn parka of yours, there are only two choices."

Guy said: "We could order a pizza." Buddy stared at Guy, watching him process what he had just said. It took quite a bit of time before he said: "Oh, right. No need to make a federal case about it, man!"

Buddy said: "I just worry about you sometimes is all. It must be hard work living in that brain of yours."

Guy said: "Yeah, you think you are so smart, like you don't want any pizza."

Buddy said: "Just because I want some pizza doesn't make me think we can get some pizza. Things don't work that way."

Guy said: "So you say. I think if we think hard enough, we could figure something out."

Buddy said: "Like what? How the hell are we going to get pizza? Send the pizza place a letter two days ago when we thought of it today?"

Guy said: "I don't know, maybe. Why not? I mean, you don't just have to give up all the time and then wait for something to come along, you know. There are options in the world. You're always so negative. It's like you give up first and then wait for something better to come along. How is that any way to live?"

Buddy said: "Well okay, Sherlock, what is your brilliant idea for getting us a pizza?"

Guy said: "I don't know, it's windy as shit, maybe other people are ordering pizzas, maybe we wait by the window and maybe a guy comes by to drop off a pizza for somebody else, then we run out and see if he will bring us a pizza back? It's not the worst idea."

Buddy said: "You know what, okay. Let's do it."

Guy said: "You serious?"

Buddy said: "Yeah, I'm very serious. If you really think this is a possibility, who am I to stop you?"

Guy said: "I don't know, if it doesn't work you will call me a bunch of names and make me feel stupid for no reason."

Buddy said: "Well, it's a stupid idea."

Guy said: "See! You're already doing it!"

Buddy said: "Alright! Jesus. What do you want from me?"

Guy said: "I want you to commit to the idea. Nothing more, nothing less."

Buddy said: "Okay, so really, all I have to do is let you try to get a pizza somehow and that will make you feel better?"

Guy said: "No, you dick. You decide it is possible to get a pizza with no phone and no electricity and then, if, if! it doesn't happen, you don't call me an idiot. That is all I ask."

Buddy said: "How is that a thing? I can just go back into my room and go back to sleep, and you can get your fantasy pizza all on your own. It changes nothing for me."

Guy said: "That's my point! Anything is possible. Do whatever you want to do, just leave me alone about it."

Buddy said: "And what if I'm wrong?"

Guy said: "It doesn't matter. That's what I mean, you sit around all day like some depressed bump on a log for no reason at all and then you take your bad feelings out on me for some reason and I'm sick of it. Shit sucks already, who needs an asshole to point that out? You think I am an idiot, take a look at yourself, man. How much energy you waste on being negative, making me feel bad, imagine if you put that energy into something good? Like, I don't know, not being a dick."

Buddy said: "Hey, man, you're kind of getting aggressive here, why is it my fault you have stupid ideas?"

Guy said: "My ideas ain't stupid, fucker."

Buddy said: "Prove it."

Guy said: "That's what I'm saying."

Buddy said: "That's what I'm saying."

Guy said: "Nuh-huh, you are saying I'm stupid for even trying."

Buddy said: "Nuh-uh also, all I am saying is your ideas are idiotic and not worth doing, whether you try them or not is beside the point."

Guy said: "What? That's the same exact thing!"

Buddy said: "It's not! You're saying your ideas are good and worth trying. I am saying your ideas suck and you can try them all you want but they won't work because even trying them is stupid."

Guy said: "You're just trying to confuse me. Fuck you. I'm gonna do it, and there is nothing you can say about it."

Buddy said: "Be my guest, what the hell do I care? I will just hang around doing nothing, and then when you fail, we can eat some eggs or peanut butter and jelly, shit, you can even pick."

Guy said: "Nope. Won't work. The stakes are too low. If I am right and get us a pizza, then you have to eat your pizza with fried peanut butter on top of it."

Buddy said: "Yeah, okay. And if I am right?"

Guy said: "If you're right then we get no pizza and we both lose."

Buddy said: "Bullshit! How is that fair at all? It's your stupid idea, there has to be stakes for you too."

Guy said: "Okay, then. What do you suggest?"

Buddy said: "Okay, let me think."

Buddy thought for a minute. He was quite invested now in making Guy regret thinking things weren't as bad as they were. He wanted to really make him suffer because of his optimism. His belief that life and living was somehow a positive thing. There was nothing bad to think of, though. All the bad stuff had already happened. They were locked in some sort of middle space where nothing could get much worse. For a second Buddy thought about making Guy give him a blanket, or his parka, but that seemed like it went a little too far. Their collective misery was already enough. Buddy realized he was being mean with his revenge fantasies. His desire to make Guy feel horrible for not giving in to how miserable things had become. He decided on the same sort of retribution that Guy had decided for Buddy.

Buddy said: "Alright, you have to eat a fried peanut butter and jelly and fried egg sandwich."

Guy said: "Done!" He held out his hand for Buddy to shake. Buddy shook his hand. Guy said: "No take backs!"

Buddy said: "Good luck."

He laughed. Suddenly he felt awful. He realized he was shaking Guy's hand while wearing the mittens the Guy had tricked him into taking. Maybe he was a bad person? Always negative, always taking, never giving? Their eyes were locked. Guy's brown empty orbs staring back at him. Like a very loyal dog receiving a treat for something he didn't understand he was doing. It was too easy for Buddy. Manipulating his friend. But was he actually manipulating him? Was this not entirely Guy's idea? It was just so stupid. Really? He would catch some pizza guy driving down the street and get them a pizza? Buddy was positive that it wouldn't work. There was no way it would work. How could it work? They couldn't even get out the front door, how was Guy going to possibly do the thing he thought he was going to do? It was almost insane. But Guy was certain it was possible. And it made Buddy sad to think that Guy was so delusional that something like that could happen. How did he think it would go down? Would he just stand by the door, looking out the window, waiting for a pizza guy to come down the street? Or would he do something else? Go out on the street, the wind blowing his stocking cap off, his parka flapping in the breeze, waving down any car that came by, asking them to go get a pizza for them? Buddy knew that Guy was like a dog. That he was very simple-minded. And once he put his mind to something, he was capable of things that normal people couldn't do, not because he was good at them, or even thought things through to the end, but by sheer will alone, which was a thing that Buddy respected, the idea of closing your eyes and just barreling through things, but this idea, this idea of getting a pizza, with no connection to the outside world, it was one of the most stupid things Buddy could think of. And Guy would have to be a true genius in his idiocy to pull it off. Buddy was not worried about having to eat fried peanut butter off of the pizza. Because there was no way in hell a pizza was ever going to enter their apartment. Not today, at least.

Guy walked over to the front door. He stood behind the ancient television that had no electricity. He opened the curtains. So he could look out. Buddy followed him into the living room. He laid down on the couch. Wanting to watch how things unfolded. Guy stood there, like a dog, looking out. Buddy could see trees getting blown in one direction. From the wind. There was a pine tree and an aspen tree. Both at hard angles. The aspen was leafless, boney and white. The pine tree was young and some of the branches made a human-like figure that was kind of begging for answers. Like it was praying for deliverance. Like it almost felt the wind blowing on it. Saying, "Please?" almost. Buddy was enjoying himself. He couldn't see what Guy was seeing, just the trees, but he assumed that nothing was happening on the street because Guy kept looking out like a dog, ready to mobilize when something he thought would make the thing he thought would happen happen. Buddy was almost gleeful about this.

Periodically he would say: "How's it going there, Guy?"
Guy would say: "You'll see! Oh, here we go! Or maybe not."

Then another while would go by and Buddy, lying down on the couch, watching the wind blow the trees would say: "How 'bout now?" And Guy would keep looking out, like a dog, ready to run out. And then nothing would change. Buddy would chuckle to himself. Lying there on the couch. His hands in Guy's mittens, watching Guy acting like a dog. Buddy was impressed that Guy didn't give up. That Guy was so invested in making this thing happen. That he really thought he could just will a pizza out of thin air. When for weeks the two of them had been suffering without power, without heat, barely surviving on eggs and peanut butter and jelly because the rats out back would attack any other food they brought into the house because it would need to be kept cold and they didn't have the refrigerator to keep it cold, so they could only eat peanut butter and jelly sandwiches and fried eggs. And Buddy, who thought this sucked, never once thought that there was any other option. Especially the option, or idea, of getting a hot pizza delivered to the front door, whether it was from sending a letter to the pizza place or not, at any point in time, which itself was an insane idea, but still, the idea that Guy could flag a pizza guy down just because the wind was blowing so hard and maybe, just maybe, he could also get the pizza guy to go back and get another pizza and bring it back? Buddy wasn't cold while this was happening because he was thoroughly entertained by it all. Guy was a fool. A dum-dum of all incursions. What kind of idiot would even think this was a possibility?

It was an insane thing that happened next. Buddy was drifting off to sleep. Watching Guy look out the window. Like a dog. The two trees at very odd angles to the wind. Guy turned the knob of the door. The door opened a little and a gush of wind came in. Guy opened it further and a guy came in. He was holding a pizza in a thermal bag. The screen door whacking against the building. The guy said: "This you guys?" Guy backed up, giving the guy some space. The wind had disoriented him. He was glad to be inside.

Guy said: "It is." Buddy shot up. He couldn't believe it.

Buddy said: "It's not! That's not our pizza!"

The guy said: "I don't give a shit, it's yours or somebody else's! I can't take this shit!"

Guy said: "Pay the guy, Buddy." Buddy stood up.

Buddy said: "No! No way in hell!"

The pizza guy said: "Take it or leave it, dude, your choice. I'm not going back out there, fuck that!"

Guy said: "Pay the dude, fucker!"

Buddy said: "Yeah, fine!" He pulled the wad of rent money out of his front pocket and handed the pizza guy a twenty. The pizza guy took the pizza out of the thermal bag and handed it to Guy.

The pizza guy said: "I don't got change."

Buddy said: "Yeah, well, merry fucking Christmas."

Guy said: "Thanks, man!"

The pizza guy said: "Enjoy!" He ran out back to his car. The wind attacking him like he was going to fly down the street. Guy held the pizza in his hands and managed to shut the front door. Buddy stood there putting the rent money back in his front pocket. Baffled by what had just happened. Guy was smiling. He turned the pizza box around so he could open it. He said: "Pepperoni and cheese, nice."

Buddy said: "That doesn't count, man."

Guy said: "Like hell it doesn't."

[10]

Guy took the pizza into the kitchen. He was singing a song: "Pizza, pizza, pizza! Oh, some tasty pizza! Don't you want some pizza? Hot and tasty pizza? I do! Do you? I'm sure you do! How do you like your pizza? Pizza, pizza, pizza! I like-a pepperoni and fried peanut butter pizza, yum, yum, indeed!" He put the pizza on the counter. Opened the lid, took a great big whiff and shut the lid again. Buddy had followed him into the kitchen.

> Guy said: "I tell you what! That is some good smelling pizza! Too bad you are about to ruin it for yourself!"
>
> Buddy said: "You can't be serious."
>
> Guy said: "Serious as cancer, dum-dum. Who is the dum-dum now?"
>
> Buddy said: "You're still the dum-dum, because I ain't frying up no peanut butter to eat no pizza."
>
> Guy said: "Well, that's fine by me, but you ain't getting no tasty pizza if you don't."
>
> Buddy said: "Yeah, who's gonna stop me?"
>
> Guy said: "You're looking right at him."
>
> Buddy said: "You and what army?"
>
> Guy said: "Dude, I would rather this pizza go to the rats before you get a single slice without peanut butter on it."

Buddy said: "C'mon! You're that stupid?"

Guy said: "See! See what I mean? You're a dick all day long and then when I am right, you treat me like a jerk? Yeah, fuck you. I am that stupid, dickwad."

Buddy said: "C'mon! We can't ruin a perfectly good pizza!"

Guy said: "I ain't ruining shit. My pizza will be just fine."

Buddy said: "Yeah, but..."

Guy said: "A deal's a deal, man, you would have done the exact same thing if I had lost. And you would have been glad about it."

Buddy said: "Yeah, but that was before we had pizza!"

Guy said: "I don't make monkeys, I just train them."

Buddy said: "What the fuck does that mean?"

Guy said: "You know what I mean."

Buddy said: "I don't know what you mean. Are you really going to deny me pizza?"

Guy said: "I ain't denying you shit, fry up some peanut butter, brother, let's get this feast going!" Guy started singing his pizza song again.

Buddy said: "Are you really willing to fight me about this? I can just take that pizza and go into my room."

Guy said: "Try me."

Buddy reached for the box. Guy slapped his hand. Buddy backed away. He looked at Guy. Guy was smiling. Then he cocked his head to the side. In a way that mocked Buddy. Suggesting that if he tried to get the pizza again, he would get the same result. Buddy reached for the pizza again. Guy slapped his arm hard this time. This made Buddy upset. The slap hurt. He lunged for the pizza. Guy grabbed Buddy's upper body. They fell to the floor wrestling. Guy's face went under the cabinets, his lip pressing against the edge of the wood. There was hair and dirt all over the linoleum. The floor smelled like pine mixed with dog shit. Guy wrapped his legs around Buddy. Started squeezing. Buddy was pushing Guy's face into the cabinet. Guy elbowed Buddy's head. His stocking cap came off. Guy bit Buddy's mittened fingers. Buddy yelped. He started punching at Guy. But because Guy had him trapped between his legs he couldn't connect. Guy grabbed Buddy's bald head and started slapping it. Buddy yelled: "What the fuck are you doing?!" Guy yelled: "You're my bongo, bitch!" Buddy somehow reached under Guy and grabbed his genitals. Guy screamed and let his legs loose. Buddy rolled free and stood up. His eyes were missing their pupils. Green orbs with barely a pinprick of black. His jaw was set and a little trickle of blood was running out of his nostril. He looked like he was about to dive onto Guy. Who was lying on the linoleum, his head leaning against the cabinets, assorted hairs and dirt hanging from his chin. His eyes were pure black. He was waiting for Buddy to dive. He had every intention of thumbing his eyes out. Buddy saw the look in Guy's eyes and cowarded. He took a quick glance at the pizza box on the counter. Looked back at Guy. Guy was now showing teeth. Buddy wiped his nose with his mittened hand. He looked at his hand. The red blood on the black mittens. He couldn't take it. He ran to his room and shut the door. He fell onto his bed and started crying. A crying that was so big and so unexpected and so vulnerable and so miserable and so intense that Buddy was on the verge of vomiting. He cried himself into a ball on top of his flimsy blankets. Kicking his feet out whenever a big wail came. He didn't know why he was such a loser. Why he couldn't get a tasty slice of pizza without Guy giving him so much trouble, why nothing ever worked out for him, how he couldn't pay the rent or even the electric bill. How he was just so stupid and alone. A loser doing nothing but loser things all the time. He wanted to punch himself because he was so stupid. He would never get ahead. And he just wanted some pizza, but Guy was being a huge jerk about it. Buddy cried and cried. His head cold and his mittens, the trick mittens that he had stolen from Guy, wiping his tears away. His nose hurt and he wished he was dead.

At the same time, Guy was getting up from the linoleum floor. Wiping detritus from his face. His face hurt. The box of pizza making him want to punch it. His small victory not worth the trouble it had caused. He walked to Buddy's door and listened to him bawling. He was about to knock on the door but changed his mind. Guy went back to the kitchen and stood there looking at the pizza box. This made him feel bad for Buddy. He took two plates from the cupboards and set them next to the pizza box. He opened the box. Put a slice on both plates. He walked to Buddy's room and kicked the door. He said: "Open up!" Buddy stopped sobbing. A moment went by. Guy said: "Dude, you gotta open the door!" Guy heard some movement then the door cracked open. Guy pushed the door open further with his foot. Buddy was lying on the bed. His back to Guy.

Guy said: "Hey, man, here. I didn't mean to hurt your feelings. C'mon, the shit's still warm."

Buddy said: "No, man, you are right. I don't deserve it. I'm the dum-dum."

Guy said: "You're not the dum-dum, I am the dum-dum for calling you a dum-dum! C'mon! Eat the pizza."

Buddy said: "I'm too stupid for pizza."

Guy said: "No, man! You're not too stupid for pizza! You're smart as hell for pizza! I am the idiot about pizza! I should have just let it go."

Buddy said: "But you are right, though, man. I'm a jerk. I don't mean to be a jerk, I just can't help it. I'm a loser who can't help being a jerk."

Guy said: "Ah, c'mon, no reason to be so hard on yourself. Let's just forget all about it. Here, just eat some pizza, it'll make you feel better."

Buddy sat up. He turned around and was now sitting on the bed. Guy handed him the plate with the pizza slice on it. Buddy put the plate on his lap. He picked up the slice of pizza and took a tiny pathetic bite. He chewed slowly, like a sad turtle. He looked like a turtle. His shaved head and pointy lips. His teeth showing on the sides of his mouth. Like he was trying to smile, or at least pretending to smile. The pizza was amazing though. His swollen eyes brightened. He wiped snot from the tip of his nose with the mittens. He looked at the mittens. Took them off and handed them back to Guy. Buddy said: "Here, take your gloves back, I don't know how I tricked you into giving me these, but it wasn't a nice thing to do." Guy took the gloves. He put his plate of pizza on the bed. Next to Buddy. He didn't want to take the gloves. He had tricked Buddy into taking them and he wanted Buddy to have them, but Guy also knew that Buddy was doing something grand here, the gesture was important to him. Guy would have to figure out another way to trick Buddy into taking them again. Guy put the mittens on. He wanted to tell Buddy that they were glove/mittens, not just gloves like Buddy had just called them, but he repressed this desire. He folded the mitten parts back. Exposing his fingers. He picked up his plate of pizza and sat down next to Buddy on the bed. He took a bite of pizza. The pizza was amazing. It wasn't warm anymore, but that didn't matter. He looked over at Buddy who was taking another bite of pizza, a bigger bite this time. One that involved pepperoni.

> Guy said: "Damn good pizza!"
>
> Buddy agreed: "It's pretty fucking good, man. I really can't believe it, though."
>
> Guy said: "I'm telling you, man, you can't just be so negative all the time. There are other things in this world than just doom and gloom. You need to open your eyes a little."
>
> Buddy said: "Yeah, I don't know about that, but I won't lie, I am very impressed with what just happened. It was a goddamned miracle of epic proportions, I mean, really."

This compliment came as a surprise to Guy. He was overcome with emotions. He tried to stop himself but he couldn't. He started crying. Buddy didn't notice. He was too busy eating the pizza and thinking about how crazy it was that Guy had lured a pizza from the ether. Out of the corner of his eye he noticed the Guy wasn't eating his pizza.

> Buddy said: "Why aren't you eating your pizza?"

He looked from Guy's pizza plate to Guy's face. Tears were streaming down his face. His bottom lip was trembling. Buddy put his lips into a straight line. Bracing. He really did not like to see somebody experiencing emotions. He very badly wanted to stand up and leave the room. But, like Guy before, when he wanted to tell Buddy that the glove/mittens were not just gloves, like Buddy had said, Buddy forced his instincts back into his body and said: "Why are you crying?"

Guy tried very hard to stop crying. He couldn't speak. He was inundated with emotion. He didn't like to see his best buddy in the world being sad, and he wasn't used to being complimented for things he had done. His entire body was tingling. He was insanely proud and insanely sad at the exact same time. Guy was fighting both of these emotions at the same time. In the end the pride lost out. It was such a queer emotion that it was the easier of the two to dismiss. A fluke of an emotion. A thing that somehow Buddy was able to articulate, verbally, and a thing that Guy was not able to use his words to describe. Buddy was the kind of guy that bragged about his victories even when they weren't victories. He was also the kind of guy that could express his frustrations with the world. With words. Buddy was actually quite simple. He was a simple man. A very boring man really, he had no inner workings. Everything he was was there on the outside to be seen. He had no secret thoughts. He said the things that he thought, whether it was good for him or not. And it wasn't something odd about him, or something innate and uncontrollable. Buddy could have easily not said anything he ever said. He didn't have some sort of body issue or brain issue that forced his thoughts out of his mouth, he simply, merely, thought that the world wanted to hear what he thought of it. Meaning the world. Buddy, for the most part, was in control of his body and mind, whether his mind and body were something worth reflecting upon is a different matter altogether, but Buddy, he said what he thought and he thought what he said and he didn't think about it either way. He had complete confidence that the world needed to hear what was going on in his mind and heart. Guy on the other hand was quite different. He had a layer of film over every thought and emotion he experienced. And it wasn't like he was hiding things from the world, he just didn't think what he thought and felt really mattered to anyone but himself. And for the most part he wasn't wrong about that. In a very big sense, nothing he thought or felt mattered in the least. Especially when it came to his feelings. But there were moments—moments when the film that separated his thoughts and emotions from the real world, the actual world—where he became struck by a certain amount of clarity, when he became like Buddy. When it didn't matter what anyone thought or did, when he could just be open and not convoluted. Moments when his heart and his head would expand at the same time, allowing him to think clearly, to emote clearly, when all the thing he had hidden behind that film of thought, that film of existence, that film of self-identity, when that film became clear as water and allowed Guy to be as honest and intelligent and forthright as he actually was. Deep down. In his heart and deep down in his brain. And that was the thing. Guy was actually much smarter than Buddy. Both intellectually and emotionally, he just didn't have the idiotic confidence that Buddy did. To float on the surface like Buddy did. Being raised in a racist town with brown skin and black eyes had created some sort of weird skin under his already discriminated against skin. A second layer of protection. But that was only part of it. Guy was not typical. He understood things in a different way than most people. And because of this he spent all of his life fighting against people like Buddy, people that believed you should just throw whatever you had to offer the world against the wall of Society and see what clung there. Guy did not do that. He held onto everything he had. Kept it hidden from view. And then, sometimes, when something would shake his heart loose, something like a compliment couched in an insult would come around, the film would evaporate, and Guy would finally allow himself to experience the world head-on. And this time, this time the compliment was not couched in an insult, it was couched in his very sincere feelings for his best friend in the world, Buddy, and how Buddy was too sad for the world, because he was lonely and alone and didn't know where to turn, but at the same time not actually understanding that Guy was right there with him, fighting for him, and it was an odd moment, both for Guy and for Buddy, because really, Guy, sure, he was smarter and way more savvy than Buddy, emotionally or otherwise, but Guy also was not a very good communicator in the sense that, sure, he was in many, many ways not as smart as Buddy was, in ways that counted with regards to Society, but these moments, moments that were infrequent and startling when they came around, they shifted the entire notion of what a relationship was, and the hierarchy of intelligence in the world, in Society, even on such a small scale as one buddy trying to make another buddy feel better about being a complete and total asshole, when Guy felt the entire nature of living and what it meant to be alive and Buddy squirming, not wanting to have anything to do with it, because Buddy was quite simple. A simple man. A child even. And Guy, Guy was complex and had thoughts that he didn't express, and could easily be dismissed as a fool, because in many ways he was an absolute fool, he had some very foolish thoughts and a very foolish viewpoint on the world. For instance he thought Buddy was a genius, which he very much was not, but that did not matter. What Guy actually thought about the pragmatic nature of the world was not important, because deep down, down inside what it was that made Guy, Guy was something special. He was sincere. And being sincere was something that nobody could measure. And since it was a thing unmeasurable it never was acknowledged. But when it did get acknowledged, like when Buddy gave Guy a compliment for doing something that was absolutely unknowable and insanely impressive, which unleashed a series of emotions that Guy was incapable of processing, instead of merely feeling good about himself for one brief moment, Guy, a guy that was actually an emotional genius, couldn't take that compliment as a victory, because that was just too much, too complicated, too antithetical and discordant to his normal thinking and behaving, so much so that he would just ignore it altogether, because that was the easier thing to do, because it didn't require any extra thought. So, Guy, after cramming all of these things inside him that were behind that film that existed, created by Society and experience, he pushed this complicated and ineffable thought process back inside his body and heart and mind and sat there blubbering waiting for his emotions to go away so he could speak.

Guy said: "I just feel so sad that you are sad."

And Buddy, being the true idiot that he was, he took no moment to reflect on what was actually happening. He wanted to stand up and walk back to the kitchen and get another slice of pizza, maybe heat it up in the oven. But now he had to deal with this dribbling baby, unironically forgetting that he had just been crying on his bed, feeling sorry for himself, his best friend bringing a slice of pizza into his room, to make him feel better, abdicating any responsibilities to the agreement they had made before, where Buddy was supposed to fry up some peanut butter and eat it on the very same pizza that Guy had brought into the room to make him feel better with. Like this was a thing that didn't just happen mere moments before. No, Buddy did not understand this or even try to understand this. Instead, he did something that knocked Guy out of his ruminations, and who knows, maybe it was for the best? Whether Guy was an emotional genius or not, it maybe did not matter, because really, in the end it was two buddies eating pizza on a mattress without power in their apartment, unable to pay the rent, and experiencing a windfall in epically weird proportions, a thing that was not only unexpected but genius in its own way. Buddy saw the thing as it was. He responded to this very simple way of seeing things like he always saw things. And being afraid of any emotion that came out of his body or mind, he simply bullied Guy for no reason at all. That is, unless bullying could be considered an emotion. A way to defer pain until you felt better about yourself until something more painful came along.

Buddy said: "Oh, great, here come the waterworks."

This statement alone reset the two roommates, the two best buddies in the world's relationship. Where one guy was an absolute asshole and the other one was an emotional genius. Where one of the guys was absolutely brave and open to anything the world would throw at them, and the other one was a complete coward afraid of his own farts. Startled by noises that came from behind him. And since Guy was so open, so sincere, he took Buddy straight-on. In good reckoning, good faith even.

> Guy said: "Yeah, I know, I know, I need to be cool, man." Guy wiped his nose with the mitten/gloves. He took another bite of pizza. It was cold but amazing.
>
> Buddy said: "Come on! Let's go heat up the pizza in the oven!"
>
> Guy said: "You sure you're alright?"
>
> Buddy said: "Don't worry about me, man. I'm fine!"
>
> Guy said: "You sure?"
>
> Buddy said: "I'm fine!"
>
> Guy said: "You sure? I worry about you, is all."
>
> Buddy said: "Drop it, dog."
>
> Guy said: "Yeah, okay."
>
> Buddy said: "You don't believe me? Look! I can do a pizza dance! Even sing your dumb song!"

Buddy danced while holding his plate out in front of himself.

He sang: "Pizza, pizza, pizza! We got some tasty pizza! Yum, yum, yum! Put it on my tongue! What's that? You got some fried peanut butter sizzlin'? You got some questions I been quizlin'? I got the answer. Pizza, pizza, pizza! I got the answer. Why didn't you pants-her? I would like to see her panties, her panties and her aunties. Pubic hair, how do you dare?"

This cheered Guy up.

Buddy said: "Satisfied?"
Guy said: "I guess."
Buddy said: "C'mon! I'm hungry. Let's go heat the shit up again. No reason we should be eating cold pizza, my friend!"

They went into the kitchen. Both of them holding their plates. Buddy's slice of pizza was eaten. Guy was still eating his. It was cold but delicious. Buddy looked down. His stocking cap was on the floor. He picked it up and brushed it off. He put it back on. Covering his ears. He turned the oven on. Set it to broil. The gas bill was so small that even though they hadn't paid it in forever, it would probably be another few months before it was turned off.

As they stood there waiting for the oven to heat up Guy said: "We're idiots, Buddy! Why don't we just open the oven and heat ourselves that way? It's not like they are going to shut the gas off anytime soon, right?"
Buddy said: "I don't know. I don't remember paying that bill, but you're right though! We are idiots!"

Buddy opened the oven. The heat coming out of it was great. They stood there warming their hands like a couple of hobos standing next to a trash fire.

Buddy said: "Why didn't we think of this before?!"
Guy said: "I don't know, but this is great!"

He took the mitten/gloves off and put them in his parka pockets. His pants felt warm now. Both of their pants felt warm now. They were standing on either side of the stove door. Warming themselves. Smiling. Both of them turning around and getting their backs warm. Like rotating chickens on a spit. When the heat coming from the oven seemed hot enough, Guy opened the pizza box and put two slices of pepperoni pizza onto the rack. They stood there watching it get warm. Then hot. Then the pizza started cooking. The pepperoni sizzling. They pulled their slices out. To each, their own. Blowing on the tips. Taking an exploratory bite. Their knees now getting hot. They both backed away and ate the pizza. Smiling at each other. Thinking they were geniuses for discovering warmth. Like they had discovered fire. The pizza was great. Both of them wanted another slice.

Buddy said: "Let's hold on with the rest, right? We'll prolly want it later, right?"

Guy didn't agree. He wanted more pizza now. There were four slices left. The wind kicked up again. Started blowing against the backside of the apartment.

Guy said: "Yeah, I suppose."
Buddy said: "What? You disagree?"
Guy said: "I don't know, I'm still hungry is all."
Buddy said: "I can fry you up an egg."
Guy said: "Yeah, but what's the point of pizza if you can't eat it?"
Buddy said: "I don't know, but later would be better, right?"

Guy said: "I guess, but..."

Buddy said: "Yeah, but don't you want a nice treat for later?"

Guy said: "I don't know, it kind of sucks either way, I guess."

Buddy said: "Oh, so now you are the negative dude? I don't know, what do they call that? Delayed gratification?"

Guy said: "About pizza? Nothing is going to change, man. We either eat this pizza now, or we eat it later, I mean, I don't know, I kind of want to eat it now."

Buddy said: "But then what?"

Guy said: "I don't know, we got eggs."

Buddy said: "But eggs suck."

Guy said: "Yeah, but it seems weird to not just eat the pizza, I mean, why not?"

Buddy said: "I don't know, maybe we want pizza later?"

Guy said: "Yeah, but I want pizza now."

Buddy said: "Yeah, okay, fine! Throw two more slices in. You'll regret it later."

Guy said: "When? When we don't have any more pizza? When we have to eat eggs? Seems like we have to do that anyway, why make a middleman out of everything? It's not like we are starving. Why not live a little?"

Buddy said: "Alright, enough with the yack-attack, dude."

Guy smiled. He had won the argument. This confused him. He wasn't used to winning arguments, and now he had won two in just one day. And after Buddy's break-down, he had taken the role of big brother. Everything was suddenly upside-down. This made him nervous. Full of self-doubt. What had changed? What was he missing? He tried to think through it. Buddy interrupted his thinking.

He said: "What's the hold up?"

Guy said: "I don't know, I'm thinking."

Buddy said: "About what? Pizza? I told you, I agree with you now."

Guy said: "Yeah, that's weird though."

Buddy said: "What's so weird about agreeing about pizza?"

Guy said: "It's not that. It's just." Guy couldn't find the words he wanted to use. If he said the wrong thing Buddy would mock him or make him feel bad.

Buddy said: "It's just what? Spit it out."

Guy said: "I mean, what's going on." Guy paused. He showed no indication he was going to keep speaking. Buddy found this frustrating.

Buddy said: "Dude, you are being cryptic as fuck. Out with it!"

Guy said: "I mean, it's just weird. The pizza miracle, then me cheering you up, and now winning the pizza argument, what is happening? There is no way that pizza would have just shown up like that, none, and usually you are the one who cheers me up, and the pizza argument, I mean, I have never won an argument in my life. Do you think I, like, grew some superpowers or something?"

Guy instantly regretted saying the last thing. It was a tiny thought he had that he knew Buddy would mock, he didn't mean to say it out loud, but he couldn't take it back now.

Buddy said: "Yeah, you're Superman now, that is it, that explains all of it. Really? That is what's keeping you from throwing two slices into the oven?"

Guy said: "No! That is not what I am saying! I just think it's weird is all, the superpowers thing was just a thought I had."

Buddy said: "Well, it is a stupid thought. Nobody just gets superpowers, man. Maybe we should climb up to the roof and have you jump off just in case you are right?"

Guy said: "No reason to be a jerk, jerk."

Buddy said: "Sorry, I just don't understand you sometimes. Life isn't some mysterious thing where a few good things happen to you and suddenly you become like special all of the sudden. It's simple stuff, man, I mean, think about it, maybe I just want some pizza and I didn't want to admit it, that's not so strange, I mean, it's not like you convinced me, I just convinced myself when you were talking. And as far as you cheering me up, you do that all the time, it's just today I am feeling pretty lousy, I mean, this wind is driving me nuts and we need money pretty damn bad, I mean, who knows, maybe in a little while you will need me to cheer you up? It's possible. Right?"

Guy said: "And the pizza miracle?"

Buddy said: "I have to agree with you on that one, man. I still can't believe it. I mean, yeah, maybe you are right, maybe you have special powers? Maybe we can test it again without having you jump off the roof? C'mon, think of something else! Something bigger than pizza. Like money. Think up a money miracle for us."

Buddy was half-joking about this. He was quite astonished about the pizza miracle, but he didn't think it was something supernatural, but as far as Guy doing something equally astonishing with regards to money, Buddy was quite skeptical. Guy, however, took Buddy's suggestion in good faith. He thought for a second. Trying to conjure up a scheme as good as the pizza miracle, which had just come to him out of the blue. Which was a miracle on its own. Guy didn't often have practical actuating thoughts. Especially actuating thoughts that paid out. He tried to get into the mindset of when he had the pizza miracle thought. He couldn't remember what made him think it up. He decided that was important for the success of any new miracles.

Guy said: "Okay, what were we talking about when I had the idea for looking outside and waiting for a pizza guy to come around so we could flag him down and get some pizza?"

Buddy said: "I don't know, I said something smart, you said something stupid, then you got mad at me for calling what you said stupid, then I said something about proving you wrong, and you said something about proving me wrong, and then you waited by the window and I laid down on the couch and then a miracle happened. I mean, I can call you stupid if you think that will make a miracle happen?"

Guy said: "Jesus Christ, man, why are you always such a dick? No, wait! You're right, this is exactly how it happened. Okay, keep being a dick. That's the thing! You're a dick, and I am not a dick. I say something smart, and you say something mean and hurtful, that is where the magic comes from. Go on."
Buddy said: "Seriously?"

Guy looked very serious. He was convinced this was the trick. That Buddy being an abusive friend was the solution to their problems.

Buddy said: "Um, you smell bad and you use too much toilet paper and jerk off too much and you need to brush your teeth more and you're kind of stupid and you dress funny and you..."
Guy said: "No! Not insults, that is not what I mean, you have to argue with me about something I say that you think is stupid."
Buddy said: "Well, you got to say something stupid then."
Guy said: "Okay. How about..."

He stopped to think. Then he got confused, if what he was thinking was stupid then he wouldn't say it, so then Buddy wouldn't argue with him, so he had to think up something smart instead of something stupid. But then, he didn't really think like that, he never thought his ideas were stupid, he only thought that Buddy would be a jerk about the things he said, no matter if they were smart or stupid. This confused Guy.

He said: "That doesn't work. I need to think my thoughts are smart first, then you have to think they are dumb.

Percolator

Then I have to defend them, and that is how the whole thing works."

Buddy said: "Okay, so we need to wait for you to have a smart thought? I mean, it's a good thing we have all this time to kill. What with the wind and all."

Guy said: "Yeah, shut up. I'll think of something."

Buddy said: "Don't be offended if I don't hold my breath."

Guy said: "Shut it. Let's make some coffee, that will help me think."

Buddy said: "See! You're already having some whoppers. Maybe we can go fly a kite, see which way the wind blows?"

Guy said: "Ha-ha-ha. Real funny. C'mon though, I think once I have some coffee things will start percolating."

Guy stood next to the oven, warming his hands while Buddy cleaned the percolator. Dumping the used coffee grounds into the sink and rinsing them down the drain. He rinsed the carafe, and the tuna can with holes. He filled the carafe with water and put it on a burner. He lit the flame underneath it. He put fresh coffee grounds into the tuna can with holes. The interior apparatus, the stem and the tuna can with holes, stood there on the counter waiting for the water to boil. The two lids. The glass lid and the holed lid. Waiting as well. The tongs. For when Guy would tong the tuna can with holes and the stem into the carafe. Once the water boiled. After, Buddy would turn the flame off and let the boiling water rest. It was a delicate operation. Buddy felt like he was handling nuclear materials. That at any moment something could go wrong that would cause them both to be blown to smithereens.

Guy on the other side of the opened oven door was standing there trying to have a brainwave. Trying to think up something genius. His pants warm. His naked hands hovering above the heat coming out from the oven. The mitten/gloves in his parka pockets. Nothing was coming to him though. His brain wasn't working. He kept thinking the word: "Think!" Over and over again. At one point he knocked on his head, with his knuckles. He thought: "Knock-knock! Anyone home?" Then he took off his stocking cap. Rubbed his hair. Thinking this would help. This made him look at Buddy. Buddy was still working on the Bubbler. Like a scientist handling nuclear rods. Guy was glad it wasn't him that was doing that. It seemed stressful and complicated. Guy got distracted thinking about when he would have to tong the tuna can with holes into the carafe with nearly boiling water. He shook that thought off and tried to think some more. He really was getting nothing. He tried to picture money. A hundred-dollar bill. He couldn't remember what a hundred-dollar bill looked like. He tried to think of any money he could describe. Or picture in his mind. All he could think of was pennies. Abraham Lincoln. But was that true? He didn't know. He reached into his pants pocket to find some change. He didn't have any.

Guy said: "Hey, Buddy, give me a twenty, I need to visualize."

Buddy looked over. He was watching the water. Waiting for it to boil.

Buddy said: "Visualize what?"

Guy said: "Money. I can't seem to remember what money looks like."

Buddy said: "Man, I can see the smoke pouring out of your ears, I don't think visualizing money is your problem."

Guy said: "Oh, shut up. Cough it up."

Buddy didn't want to give Guy a twenty, but he also was curious about what he might do with it. He took the rent money out of his pocket and handed Guy a twenty. He put the wad back into his pocket. Making a note to himself that now two twenties were gone from their total amount. One for the pizza miracle, and now one for Guy's visualization. Buddy watched the water heating up. He also watched Guy looking at the twenty-dollar bill, trying to visualize something. Buddy was not convinced that this was a bad maneuver. Earlier when he was trying to convince Guy that he didn't actually have superpowers, Buddy did not want to admit that maybe it was true. Because what he had said was true. Guy never was right. And he never predicted anything, and he never really was the person cheering Buddy up. Buddy just couldn't admit it in the moment. Things had changed. Everything was upside down. Guy was the smart one, the older brother, the predictor of things, and it had rubbed Buddy the wrong way. He wasn't lying when he said that he was having a lousy day. The day was unfriendly. Buddy was in a bad mood. Had been all day long. From the second he had woken up. He was mad at Guy for not paying the electricity bill, but he was more mad at himself for letting things get this far, to become this poor, to not pay rent for so many months, and to be living like a loser for so long, even when he could have done something to prevent it. Buddy didn't want to admit it, but he was just as confused about things as Guy was. Maybe even more confused. So, seeing Guy hold that twenty-dollar bill to his nose, trying to visualize something, this gave Buddy a sense of hope. Like, maybe Guy would pull another trick off. Another miracle. Like the pizza miracle. Because anything was possible. As Guy had convinced Buddy. Even though Buddy hadn't given that victory to Guy. A fourth victory. The pizza miracle, the older brother thing, the pizza argument, and now, the "Anything is possible" victory. Things were upside-down for sure. And the added danger of the Bubbler, the open oven heating the kitchen, Buddy felt out of sorts. He felt small compared to Guy. Guy was something new. Like maybe he actually did have superpowers now. And that was something that Buddy could not accept. However, he wasn't foolish enough to dismiss Guy outright.

[11]

Guy visualized the money while Buddy got the Bubbler going. This was typical behavior for them. Their very odd collaboration of solving problems. It seemed to work. For them at least. They were still alive after living away from home for many years. There was also something else going on, beneath the outer oddness of their peculiar co-habitation. The problem with Guy and Buddy was simple. It was always simple. They needed money. From the day they started living together to this exact moment, they needed money. Both of them. Neither one of them could survive without the other. Not in the sense that if one of them moved out, that would be it. They would both have to move out. And it is maybe true that either one of them could live on their own, in a single bedroom apartment, or a studio, but that is unlikely. Because, although money was the problem that these two suffered from, that was not the issue that kept them poor. In fact, if left alone, either one of them would just starve to death without really thinking or doing anything about it. They would either starve to death or simply move back home. Guy with his parents, even though that was the last thing in the world that they wanted, and Buddy with his mom, even though that was the last thing in the world she wanted. And their money problem was not just a work problem. Sure, it is true that if they worked more they would have more money, but both Guy and Buddy were so very awful with money that having more money would actually work against them. They would just spend it. Not thinking about it at all. Sure, Buddy was slightly better than Guy when it came to managing money. He at least understood where his money went and tried his best not to spend his money. But he spent it anyway. Which is why working more wouldn't help them. Well, maybe now. Since things had gotten so out of control. But in order for that to work, for them to work more to get more money to pay more bills and rent, there would need to be a third person involved. Somebody that physically took the extra money they made away from them. Someone that would need to loan them the money they needed and then make sure they were working to get more money. And this person would have a full-time job on their hands. Both Guy and Buddy, who were not lazy, who enjoyed doing things, who understood that you needed money to live, they just didn't have the drive to control the things they needed to control. Like their finances, or their bills, or the rent. And as much as having more money at this exact moment may indeed have solved some of their problems, if not all of them, had you sent either of them alone to the landlord or the electrical company with a wad of cash to pay all of the debt off, neither one of them would have made it there. It just wouldn't happen. It would be exactly equal to sending Jack from the history books to town with his mother's cow. They both, both Guy and Buddy, would come back with magic beans. And yet together, however, they stood a chance in this world. Where, sure, they may not precisely enjoy having a job or want to go to work, but together, they did things to ensure their mutual existence. They would prod each other, poke, pry, they would shame each other and have moments of abject dread when the rent was due. To the point that at that moment, when things were too stressful to get through the day, in a way that they both truly understood they were teetering on some very precarious balancing device, that is when they would pull it together and figure it out. Why it hadn't happened in the last few months was easy to understand. The winter. Winter in Wyoming was exceptionally harsh. Especially in Casper, where the wind just blew and blew and time lost all meaning. The push of the mountains nearly crushing you at all times. The dry and frozen air waiting outside for you at all times. And really, had they had a car, they probably would have paid the rent. Not because they could have driven to the landlord, but because they wouldn't have been so trapped in the apartment. They would have worked more. They would have done more things. They wouldn't have just stayed inside and been miserable. But as much as the world is open and welcome to your ambitions, sometimes the gatekeeper in this world is literally a gate. A whacking screen door against the building. And maybe you, or anyone for that matter, would not really have sympathy for these two, because life is hard and we all have to live it, but consider this before you make that final assessment. Guy would have paid the electric bill had it not been for the wind. Why Buddy tasked his very unreliable buddy with such an important task also had to do with the wind. Buddy didn't want to go outside either. He was not teaching Guy a lesson on responsibility, he was being selfish. He just didn't want to do it. He knew that Guy would fuck it up. It was obvious, but when you compare having a task that you find absolutely miserable to getting someone else to do it, can you tell me that you, yourself, wouldn't make the same choice? I don't know. Maybe you wouldn't. But if you think things are so very simple that Buddy should have just paid the electrical bill himself, and both Buddy and Guy should just work more, you are missing the very large and simple element that bound these two together. Yes, it is true that the bills need to be paid, yes it is true the rent needs to be paid, but what is also true, and will always be true for you and me and Guy and Buddy, it never ends. Not today, when you don't have electricity or heat or rent, or yesterday when you had a few extra dollars, or tomorrow when you are getting evicted from your apartment. The thing with Guy and Buddy, the problem of money or the lack thereof, the problem of working more, or working less, the problem of understanding the world on either their terms or on the world's terms was not so much a question of shall I or shall I not, it was more a question of which exact battles do I need to fight today? And for them, for Guy and Buddy, the last four months the question was mostly a question of getting out the front door. A thing that I think should be taken into consideration while judging them for their missteps and juvenile actions. Guy and Buddy were not bad at doing the things that life required of them, it was simpler than that: they couldn't care less about the motives of Society or their relationship to it. They didn't feel oppressed or saddened by their position in life. Sure, like anyone poor, they wished they didn't need to think about money, or work, or life, but what made them almost tragic in their approach to existence was that they lacked that one thing that almost everyone alive has in common, which is self-preservation. Both Guy and Buddy could not, and it was not for a lack of trying, connect the simple idea that one thing leads to the next thing. That you work and save money and then you have money to spend on things that keep you alive. Somewhere along the line, for both of them, this simple idea just never sunk in. And so what if it didn't? Not everyone needs to become a plumber or a securities broker, a housewife or a cop. There is no mandate from birth that you need to be anything. For most people, who they are is just the simple fact of: this is how things are done, so do them that way. And Guy and Buddy, for whatever reason, were simpatico in this way. Neither one of them ever considered the possibility that maybe what wasn't working right in this world, for them, was themselves. And for that reason, we should think that maybe, just maybe, these two were actually not a couple losers freezing in their apartment with no electricity and no rent, but maybe, and this is a very possible maybe, maybe they were actively reimagining what it meant to be alive in this very moment in time. When nothing is certain and everything is a problem. And maybe money isn't the solution. And yes, if you gave these two unlimited money and forced them to pay their bills and rent, and forced them to work, they would do it, but no matter what, no matter how hard you drilled it into them, they wouldn't change. They would still slip and flop and grease their way right back to where they always were. Which, for now, at this exact moment, was trying to do some sort of mind trick to lure money towards themselves while carefully making coffee in a thing that both fascinated and terrified them both. And whatever it was that brought these two together to make whatever choices they were making, good, bad or idiotic, it didn't matter, because at some point, way back in the annals of time, these two were let loose in the world. And they would be this way forever. No matter how hard you tried to change them. And for whatever reason, this thing they chose to do, this battle they decided was worth fighting, they would fight it until whatever end it came to.

Buddy interrupted Guy's visualizing to have him grab the tongs and put the tuna can with holes into the formally boiling water. Guy took this job so seriously that sweat sprouted from his forehead. When he was done he looked around. Confused because he was so focused just seconds before. He couldn't find the twenty-dollar bill that Buddy had given him. He checked all of his pockets. Nothing. He looked at Buddy with panic on his face. Buddy shook his head. He reached up and yanked the twenty dollar bill out from between Guy's lips. Guy let out a huge sigh. He took the twenty from Buddy and walked around the other side of the open oven door. Buddy set the flame under the Bubbler to medium-low. He was hyper-focused on turning it down when the water started shooting out from the stem of the tuna can with holes. Guy went back to visualizing. Smelling the money. Trying to do some real thinking. He was getting nothing. Nothing but tired. He had zero thoughts. He was feeling pretty good though. The heat from the oven was nice. It made his pants warm. This made him think about his genitals. Which made him think about earlier when he was mid-whack and Buddy had come into his room and ruined things. He wanted to go into his room and finish his business, but he knew Buddy would know what he was doing, so he tried to put the thought out of his mind. Buddy noticed though. Even though he was hyper-focused on the Bubbler, he could sense something was up with Guy. He looked over. Guy had put the twenty on the counter, his black eyes were blank, his erection poking out of his pants.

> Buddy said: "Jesus Christ, man! Can't you just give it a rest?"
>
> Guy said: "What? What'd I do?"
>
> Buddy said: "Everyone can see what you did! Just go take care of it."
>
> Guy said: "I can't! You clogged me up."
>
> Buddy said: "You don't look clogged."
>
> Guy said: "I'm clogged, I can feel it."
>
> Buddy said: "How is that my fault?"
>
> Guy said: "You can't just bust in on a guy during operations, man, it's not good for the pipes."
>
> Buddy said: "Bullshit. You whack it all the time."
>
> Guy said: "Your mom whacks it all the time."
>
> Buddy said: "Your mom doesn't need to whack it."
>
> Guy said: "Oh, yeah, why is that?"
>
> Buddy said: "Why whack it when you can suck it?"

Guy said: "Your mom sucked the rust off a chrome bumper."

Buddy said: "Chrome doesn't rust, idiot."

Guy said: "Well, your mom joined a hotdog eating contest and did it in reverse."

Buddy said: "What? Like she just threw up hotdogs?"

Guy said: "No! She put them up her butt."

Buddy said: "Well, your mom showed up early to the hotdog contest and sucked all the hotdogs so much that it became a hotdog skin eating contest because she loves to suck hotdogs so much."

Guy said: "Well, your mom won the hotdog eating contest because she had the hotdog guy put the hotdogs through a portable glory hole and she couldn't get enough of them."

Buddy said: "Well, too bad for your mom because she got disqualified from the hotdog eating contest because earlier in the day she gave me a blowjob and her throat was too stretched out so they said she was cheating."

Guy said: "I heard it was the opposite. That she couldn't compete because her throat was too tiny to compete."

Buddy said: "You just said your mom couldn't compete in the hotdog competition because she was sucking my dick!"

Guy said: "No sir! I said your dick was so small my mom, oh, shut up!"

Buddy said: "Haha! Your mom sucked my dick!"

Guy said: "She didn't suck your dick, she thought it was a toothpick."

Buddy said: "Nope. She thought it was a Waterpik because of all the cum that was shooting between her teeth."

Guy said: "Don't be gross."

Buddy said: "Where have I heard that before?"

Guy said: "When your mom told you to put your skid-marked underwear in the hamper?"

Buddy said: "Only before your mom licked my chocolate stains before she licked my balls."

Guy said: "Okay! Too far!"

Buddy said: "She said that after that!"

Guy said: "Unlikely. More like, is it in yet?"

Buddy said: "Shit! The thing's bubbling. Get ready."

Guy went around to the other side of the open oven door. They watched the water percolate. The clear bubbles turning to black. When it was time, Guy put the holed lid on top of the tuna can with holes on top of the stem. He put the second lid on. Buddy turned the flame off. They both let out a sigh of relief. The apartment didn't explode. Guy rinsed out the sexy mugs. His erection was long gone. The jokes about moms had put an end to it. It was true that Buddy had clogged Guy up. But nothing was lost. He could get there eventually. And maybe he would think about Buddy's mom. Out of spite. She was attractive. And Guy had a very specific memory of her wearing some very odd and revealing khakis from a while ago that he could access in his brain. Guy smiled to himself when he thought about this. Buddy knew what he was thinking. Because Buddy was just as perverted as Guy was.

Buddy said: "Dude, don't even do it."

Guy said: "I'm gonna, you can't stop me."

Buddy said: "I got that picture of your mom in the bikini, dude, you do my mom, I do yours."

Guy said: "You do not! I got that picture back."

Buddy said: "Did you?"

Guy said: "I must have!"

He took off running to his room. Buddy followed him. Guy went to his stash of pictures that he had in a shoebox next to his bed. He rifled through them. The picture of his mom in a bikini wasn't there. He looked up at Buddy. Who was standing in the doorway smiling.

Guy said: "Where is it, man? Don't do me like that!"

Buddy said: "Relax. I'm just fucking with you."

Guy said: "Show me!"

Buddy said: "Show you what? That I don't have the photograph? How can I un-prove something?"

Guy said: "Get!"

He marched Buddy into his own room to find the photo that Buddy didn't have. Buddy had his own shoebox of photos. He went around to the other side of the bed and pulled them out. He put the box on top of the mattress and started placing them on top of the covers.

Buddy said: "Nope, nope, nope, not this one, nope, nope."

They were all pictures of Buddy and his family. After a while he found one that he hid from Guy.

Buddy said: "This is it!"

He pretended to whip his penis out and start whacking off.

Buddy said: "So hot! Look at those nipples! And the camel toe! So hot!"

Guy jumped over the back of Buddy. Grabbing the photo from him. It was a picture of Buddy with a dog that Guy didn't know about. Buddy must have been twelve years old. He looked happy. In a way that Guy had never seen Buddy look.

Guy said: "That's not my mom."

Buddy said: "Dude, I don't have a picture of your mom in a bikini, I think you may be insane."

Guy said: "You look so happy, what the hell happened to you?"

Buddy said: "Let me see that!" He grabbed the picture from Guy. "Oh, Arnold, I miss that dog. He was a good dog."

Guy said: "What? Did he die?"

Buddy said: "Yeah, Guy, all dogs die."

Guy said: "Yeah, but you seem so happy, what happened?"

Buddy said: "I don't know, the dog died and I got unhappy, what are you getting at?"

Guy said: "I don't know what I am getting at, I just feel bad that you were so happy back then."

Buddy said: "Yeah, I don't know, things suck as you get older."

Guy said: "Your mom sucks, as she gets older. Probably because she lost all of her teeth, am I right?"

Percolator

Buddy was sad. Thinking about Arnold. Looking at the picture.

Buddy said: "Yeah, probably."

Guy said: "C'mon, man, cheer up! You can remember a good dog without getting too sad, right? I got a cat that hurts my feelings."

Buddy said: "It's not just that. I got some bad feelings all around. I mean, I know you are right, but just looking at this photo, I mean, where did things go wrong?"

Guy said: "Things didn't go wrong! We are still here, fighting, man! It's not the end, we just need to stay focused!"

Buddy said: "Yeah, but poor Arnold, I mean, he never meant to do no harm, I loved that dog, and then just like all things, he was gone, it makes me feel tired."

Guy said: "Well, let's go drink some coffee then, I got some good ideas about money!"

Buddy said: "I'm not really in the mood. I think I may just sit here for a while."

Guy said: "Bullshit! Get up, man! We can't give up, just yet, we still got pizza and I have a big plan to get us out of this problem of ours!"

Buddy said: "Oh, really? You know what, never mind, I don't want to hear it, I'm not in the mood right now for your hijinks, leave me alone."

Guy said: "You serious?"

Buddy said: "Yes, I'm fucking serious, don't I look serious?!"

Guy said: "Sorry for living, no need to bite my head off, jeez. I'll leave you alone."

Buddy said: "Do it then."

Guy said: "I will."

Buddy said: "Well, what's keepin' ya?"

Guy said: "I'm leaving, just give me a second."

Buddy said: "Why are you looking at me like that?"

Guy said: "You know, you kind of look like your mom, if you put a wig on, I mean."

Buddy said: "Yeah, so?"

Guy said: "Yeah, okay, I think that's good."

Buddy said: "What's good, what the fuck are you talking about?"

Guy said: "Oh, nothing, just putting a fresh image of your mom in my bank for later."

Buddy said: "You—fucking hell! Get the fuck out of here! And take those dirty thoughts out of your mind!"

Guy said: "You can't control my mind, man! Ooh-la la, Buddy's mom, you look so great in that bikini you are wearing, care to come join me in bed?"

Buddy said: "You don't know my mom's name?"

Guy said: "I forget, that's not the point! The point is that I am going to think about bonin' your mom when I whack it in a few moments."

Buddy said: "Yeah, you want me to put on a wig and stand at the edge of your bed you sick fuck?"

Guy said: "Would you? No, that would be weird. You have a wig?"

Buddy said: "Of course I don't have a wig, dum-dum, why the hell would I have a wig?"

Guy said: "I don't know, because you are going bald? Isn't that a thing?"

Buddy said: "You're thinking of a toupée."

Guy said: "Isn't that just a wig? What's the difference?"

Buddy said: "I think a wig is for girls and a toupée is for guys."

Guy said: "Does that mean that girls have different head shapes than guys?"

Buddy said: "I don't fucking know man."

Guy said: "Come to think of it, I don't think I have ever seen a girl with a bald head. Maybe they are different? Hmmm."

Buddy said: "Goddammit! You son of a bitch, you win, okay, you win! If we are going to have this idiotic conversation let's go do it where it is warm. Fucking hell. How the hell do you even tie your shoes?"

Guy said: "I wear Velcros."

Buddy said: "Not anymore, remember? You switched back." Guy looked down at his feet.

Guy said: "Oh, right. I'm pretty good at tying my shoes. The rabbit goes around the tree, back into the hole and tighty-tighty nice and mighty."

Buddy shook his head. He stood up. He was no longer bogged down by the weight of living. Guy's inane personality had kicked him out of his funk. Now he was annoyed and wanted to stand by the oven again. His room was quite cold and the wind had picked up. He could hear it rushing against the apartment building.

Buddy said: "Out!"

Guy turned around and walked out of Buddy's room. Buddy followed him into the kitchen.

[12]

Buddy poured coffee into the two perverted cups that Guy had found somewhere at some point for some reason. The coffee was still steaming. Even after their aside in Buddy's room. Guy took the mitten/gloves from his parka pocket. He put the left-hand mitten/glove on. Handed the right-hand mitten/glove to Buddy. Guy was left-handed. Buddy was right-handed.

> Guy said: "This way we can have a warm hand when we drink the coffee. Smart right? And we can still warm our other hand with the stove."
>
> Buddy said: "That's not the worst idea you've had."

He almost said: 'Unlike your wig thoughts.' But he really didn't want to get that conversation going again. So he stopped himself from saying it. He put the mitten/glove on. Handed Guy the cup of coffee in the perverted cup. He blew on it. Took a sip and smiled. Buddy did the same thing.

Buddy said: "Okay, Einstein, let me hear your money ideas. I could use a good yuck or two."

Guy had forgotten his ideas already. The incident in Buddy's bedroom had distracted him too much. He tried to remember.

Guy said: "I can't remember now. There was something about a tennis net and a kite, but they seem to have slipped my mind. What if we just go down to the bank and ask for a loan? How hard is it to get a loan?"

Buddy said: "For most people? Probably not that hard. For us? I mean, I think you need to own stuff to get loans. Or at least have some good credit."

Guy said: "I got good credit."

Buddy said: "How do you have good credit?

Guy said: "Well, I don't owe anybody any money."

Buddy said: "You owe the landlord three months rent, if you don't count the money I have in my pocket, and you owe a bunch of money to the electrical company, I mean, right?"

Guy said: "Yeah, but I didn't borrow that money. I just haven't paid it yet."

Buddy said: "That doesn't mean you have good credit though. You have to, like, have a credit card or something to have good credit, I think you just don't have any credit."

Guy said: "You think, or you don't know? Usually, you know all about this stuff, man, what is going on with you today?"

Buddy said: "I don't know, man, I'm out of sorts. This fucking wind is driving me crazy. I can't fucking think. I want to strangle somebody."

Guy said: "Well, don't strangle me, man, I'm all you got in the world."

Buddy said: "I got my mom and my sisters and my dad."

Guy said: "Yeah, but those guys don't get you miracle pizza."

Buddy said: "Yeah, I guess."

Guy said: "You really don't think we can get a loan? We could at least try. You said it, we have to do something."

Buddy said: "Yeah, I think you have to have something to bet against, like a car or something. Or a house. They won't just give it to you if you are poor. I think you need to prove you can pay it back or something."

Guy said: "We got the apartment."

Buddy said: "Not for long. And not only that, but so what? You think the landlord is going to cosign a loan or something?"

Guy said: "What is that? Cosign?"

Buddy said: "I don't know, like put the apartment up against the loan we would take out or whatever."

Guy said: "That's a thing? Someone else can use their thing to help you get your thing?"

Buddy said: "Well, I don't know if they would put it that way, but yeah, I think."

Guy said: "Well, maybe your mom would help us cosign a loan." Buddy laughed. There was no way in hell his mom would cosign a loan for them to pay their rent and electric bills.

Buddy said: "There is no way in hell my mom would cosign a loan for us to pay the rent and electric bills. You think your parents would do that?"

Guy said: "I don't know, maybe? I mean, prolly not, but I do remember my mom, or prolly it was my dad, telling me about some sort of finance stuff at some point. I don't know, maybe this is the sort of thing they would think was a good thing for me to do?"

Buddy said: "I don't think you understand what we are talking about. I mean, no offense, because I don't know shit about this, but I don't think your parents, who seem to want nothing to do with your money situation or your living situation, who seem to, I mean, much like my mom, want nothing to do with you at all, are going to cosign a loan for you to get out of getting kicked out of this apartment or paying your electric bills. I mean, if I was them, I would think it would be a pretty lousy investment. I mean, if you can't pay your rent or electric bills, how the hell are you going to pay your rent, your electric bills, and the loan, plus there is like interest and stuff on the loan."

Guy said: "But that is the thing. The rent would then be paid. The electric bills would be paid. It would just be paying the loan back at that point. And that would just be a single thing. Not all the other stuff."

Buddy said: "Man, I really don't think you understand how money works. Or even bills for that matter. You got to pay the shit, then it keeps coming and you have to pay it again and then it keeps coming and you have to pay it again. Getting a loan just adds more paying shit to the other shit you are already paying. It's not like the need to pay the money just disappears, you have to pay that money back too. With interest."

Guy said: "Well, I am interested in paying the money back, I mean, if that is what you mean."

Buddy said: "No! It's not "interest," like you are interested in things. The money you borrow has like a percentage of money added on to it because you borrowed it. It's called interest."

Guy said: "But you can cosign your interest to somebody else?"

Buddy said: "Man, are you kidding me? This is worse than the wig conversation we were just having. You have to be joking, right?"

Guy said: "I'm not joking, we need money, can't we just borrow money? I mean, if it's all just the same anyway, why not borrow it from the bank on a cosign? You know? Make it up."

Buddy said: "Like, wait, what?"

Guy said: "I don't know, just tell the bank that my mom cosigned and then they give us the money. Who's it going to hurt? It's not like my mom would need to find out, right?"

Buddy said: "You can't just go in there and pretend you got somebody cosigning, I don't think. They need, like, documents and stuff. Papers."

Guy said: "Well, why not just make it up?"

Buddy said: "Dude, they check all that shit. You can't just walk into a bank and then say, 'Hey, this guy is like giving me permission to take money from you.'"

Guy said: "Yeah, I understand that, but it's all just paperwork, right? Why not just lie on the forms? I mean, I have all sorts of, whatever, information about my parents. I mean, if it is all just like a proof you have stuff, I mean, it's not a hard thing to get. You know what I mean?"

Buddy said: "You are talking about fraud, man. I don't know, you know? I think you go to jail for that kind of shit. You can't just make shit up."

Guy said: "Why not? What's the difference? It's all just about paying money back or something, right? What's it matter about the papers?"

Buddy said: "I don't know, man. If you want to go try and get a loan and use your parents' shit to do it without their knowledge, more power to you, but keep me out of it, I mean, I don't know what we are going to do, but committing fraud doesn't seem like the best use of our time."

Guy said: "What's the worst that could happen?"

Buddy said: "Oh, I don't know, we end up in jail."

Guy said: "Jail wouldn't be so bad. You get a nice warm cell, a nice bed, you don't have to work, they feed you. I mean, compared to what we have going now, I mean, we're going to be on the streets soon anyway, at least we could try and fight to get out of it, right?"

Buddy said: "I'm not going to jail just to pay the rent. Jail sucks. You're, like, stuck there all the time."

Guy said: "No different than this."

Buddy said: "Yeah, but you can't go outside."

Guy said: "No different than this."

Buddy said: "But you have to eat the same lousy food over and over."

Guy said: "No different than this."

Buddy said: "But you don't have the freedom to move around, like go out on the town."

Guy said: "Dude, you are describing our lives. I mean, I am not saying we break the law, but maybe? Going to jail seems better than this shit. I mean, look at us. We're warming ourselves with the fucking oven. At least jails have heat. And there prolly isn't a screen door whacking against the building all day long. And the meals have to be better than eggs or peanut butter and jelly sandwiches. And even if they are the exact same, somebody else will make them for us. And we can just lay around all day doing nothing. I mean, compared to this bullshit, jail seems like a resort town, man!"

Buddy said: "Yeah, well, I don't disagree, but I really don't think you can go into a bank and fill out some papers and they give you a bunch of money without checking into it first. Even if you know where your parents live and what their, I don't know, social security numbers are. I don't think it works that way."

Guy said: "Yeah, I understand, but what is the hurt in trying?"

Buddy said: "Like I said, be my guest, I just don't want nothing to do with it."

Guy said: "Yeah, maybe."

Buddy said: "Yeah? You're going to go try it out?"

Guy said: "I might."

Buddy said: "What's stopping you?"

Guy said: "I don't know, maybe I will wait until the wind dies down."

Buddy said: "The wind never dies down."

Guy said: "Well, maybe tomorrow then."

Buddy said: "There is no time like today."

Guy said: "Yeah, it's too much work. I would have to like, I don't know, go to my parents' house and then like, I don't know, I mean, I don't know, I'm just thinking, man!"

Buddy said: "Coward!"

Guy said: "I'm not a coward, I'm just not in the mood!"

Buddy said: "That's just what a coward would say."

Guy said: "Yeah, whatever."

Buddy said: "Bock-bock-bock! Coward in the chicken coop."

Guy said: "Man, what the hell?"

Buddy said: "What? You don't like being called a coward? Man up for a second and maybe grow some cojones."

Guy said: "What's with you? I'm constantly building you up and you are constantly cutting me down. It's kind of gross!"

Buddy said: "I'm not cutting you down, man, I am just giving it to you straight, man."

Guy said: "No, you're not, you're being a dick for no reason. My ideas aren't as stupid as you think they are.

You're just living in some dumb world where everything matches your own stupid ideas of how things should be."

Buddy said: "Dude! You can't just go to the bank and ask for money, it doesn't work that way."

Guy said: "Yeah, okay. And? So what! I am just thinking out loud, I mean, I don't think you have noticed, but we are fucked! You and me, fucked! I'm sorry, but I am a little stressed out about it. I don't want to move into the gutter, I don't. I can't move back home, I think, and if we can't get right with our bills, I am afraid we might lose our home. And it makes me sad! I don't want to move. I enjoy living here with you. Even if you think I am an idiot!"

Guy put his perverted coffee cup on the counter. He had tears running down his face. He was wearing one mitten/glove. On his left hand. Because he was left-handed. Because he was trying to figure out a way for Buddy, his best friend in the world, to get both mitten/gloves back on his hands. He was halfway there. His next move was to leave the left-handed glove on the counter for Buddy to pick it up absentmindedly. But now Guy was too upset to even do that. Guy ran into his room and slammed the door. The change in temperature was drastic. The wind and the sound of the screen door whacking against the building was depressing. Guy covered himself with his wimpy blankets. Crying into his pillow. His left hand wiping away the tears. Because that was the hand his mitten/glove was on. The hand he liked to use. Because he was left-handed.

[13]

Guy didn't cry for very long. He kind of forgot why he even went into his room. He remembered being very frustrated about money and how borrowing money went, but once he was in his room, cold and alone, he didn't feel his emotions as strongly. He spent a moment lying in bed. Kind of thinking, more like a series of unrelated images went through his head like a pinwheel. All distinctly different in subject and coloring. His mind twirled around like this until he found what he was looking for. It was Buddy's mom wearing khakis. Her tiny little butt. The pants kind of riding up it a little, just enough to give Guy feelings. He reached down and undid his pants. He pulled them down below his erection. He kept the mitten/glove on. He liked the feeling of it. The strange new feeling. He was starting to think he may not give the mitten/glove to Buddy after all. He was imagining Buddy's mom pulling down her pants, exposing her underwear, then he imagined pulling her underwear down, and, just as he was about to finish, Buddy came into the room without knocking. Guy startled.

Buddy said: "Goddammit! Again? Do you just sit around yanking your ding-dong all day? I thought you were upset? You ran in here crying like two seconds ago and now you're already pulling your pud? My god, man! I think you have a problem."

Buddy paused. A thought occurred to him, "You better not be whacking it to my mom!" Guy smiled. A great big smile.

Buddy said: "Goddammit!"

Guy said: "It was getting pretty good, man! You would have been proud, I was doing your mom quite the service and she was loving it! Wet as a walrus!"

Buddy said: "Don't be gross." Guy suddenly got a very serious look on his face.

Guy said: "Buddy?"

Buddy said: "Yes, Guy?"

Guy said: "I don't want to lose our house."

Buddy said: "I don't either."

Guy said: "What are we going to do?"

Buddy said: "I don't know."

Guy said: "I'm scared."

Buddy said: "Don't be scared, we'll figure it out. C'mon, let's go eat some pizza."

Guy said: "Give me a second."

Buddy said: "Nope! Out of bed! I will not allow you to sully my dear mother's likeness."

Guy said: "Her likeness? What does that mean?"

Buddy said: "Her image. Out! Chop-chop!"

Guy got out of bed. His erection stiff in the breeze. He shook it at Buddy.

Buddy screamed: "Put that away! You pervert!"

He turned around and walked into the kitchen. Guy pulled his pants up. He had to work to get his erection into his pants. He was about to shut the door and finish the job when Buddy yelled from the other room:

"Dude! Put it away and get your ass in here!"

Guy thought to himself: "How did he know?" He buttoned and zipped and walked into the kitchen. Buddy was putting two slices of pizza into the oven. He was using his mittened/gloved hand to do this.

Guy said: "You should try whacking off with the mitten/glove on, man. It's something else, I'm telling ya."

Buddy said: "Really?" Buddy wasn't the pervert that Guy was, but a decent suggestion is a decent suggestion no matter where it comes from. "What do you mean?"

Guy said: "I don't know, it's like the Stranger, or whatever, but different. Like a handy from a girl in a car during a snowstorm or something."

The Stranger was when you lie on your arm until it falls asleep from lack of blood flow, then when you masturbate it feels like somebody else is doing it to you. An urban myth. An urban myth that was so well-promulgated that every single teenage boy in America, maybe the entire world, knew about it. And nobody knew if it worked because nobody could get it to happen. There were times when you would fall asleep and wake up with "Dead-Arm," and maybe then try and masturbate, but that always resulted in pins and needles running up and down your arm. But the ability to make your arm go dead and then masturbate with it was a thing nearly impossible. But the myth persisted. And because it was promulgated by teenage boys, it had spanned many decades, generations, eons even. So when Guy said it was like the Stranger but different, he did not need to explain what he meant to Buddy, Buddy was well aware of the Stranger.

Buddy said: "No shit?"

He was curious now. He would surely give it a try. Later maybe. At bedtime. Although there was nothing to think about these days. They hadn't been out of the house in a while and aside from Guy's very odd nudie mag there was nothing in the house to look at. The perverted mugs and the perverted playing cards aside. And the cards didn't do it for Buddy. He wasn't like Guy. Guy could masturbate to the cards because, even though he was not gay, the mere suggestion of sex would get him aroused. And Guy also had an imagination. He could just think of things and do things with the thoughts. Buddy lacked any imagination. He needed very specific visuals to do things. And although he had used Guy's nudie mag in the past, he was too embarrassed to ask him to borrow it. He wished he had a picture of Guy's mom in a bikini like he had pretended to have before. She was a handsome lady. With a very nice set of jugs, as Buddy would describe her. Buddy was thinking of Guy's mom when Guy said: "Maybe we could get like the government to help us? Like, I don't know, don't they do, like, welfare or something?" Buddy took a second to understand that Guy wasn't talking about the mitten/glove thing anymore. He was trying desperately to conjure up an image of Guy's mom. But he was getting nowhere.

Buddy said: "What?"

Guy said: "I don't know, like food stamps, but for rent. Do they make rent stamps?"

Buddy said: "Hmmm. I mean, um, that is not a bad idea, actually. The problem though is that we are in Wyoming. I don't know for sure, but I think that is kind of looked down upon. But you're not wrong. I wonder."

Percolator

Buddy started trying to think about this idea. And like his normal self, he was suddenly an expert on the matter and was going to tell Guy all the things that he had maybe heard over his lifetime from secondhand sources as concrete facts. Facts only a well-traveled scholar would have.

Buddy said: "You see, though, we would need to prove that we are poor for a reason. Like an illness or something, like maybe one of us would have to pretend to be disabled. And then they would have to give us a social worker, I believe, if my facts are right, somebody that needs to come around and check on things, and they got guys all around taking pictures of this sort of stuff, working for the government to prove you are not disabled, so, I mean, if we were to do this, you would have to really take your acting chops up a notch or two."

Guy said: "Like I would have to pretend to have a limp or something? I could do that."

Buddy said: "All the time? Like every day. The second you left the apartment, and even prolly they would put cameras in our house so you would have to have a limp inside here too."

Guy said: "I could do that."

Buddy said: "All the time? Even if we had some hot babes over and we were drinking beer? You think you could hump with a limp?"

Guy said: "I don't hump with a limp. I'm usually pretty stiff."

Buddy said: "You joking?"

Guy said: "About what?"

Buddy said: "No, you idiot! Not a limp dick, an actual limp, like if someone was looking at the tapes and noticed you were humping like a normal person not like a disabled person."

Guy said: "How does a disabled person hump?"

Buddy said: "I don't fucking know, man! You're missing my point. You'd have to pretend to have a limp all day long, all night long, even if you got up to go to the bathroom in the middle of the night you need to have a limp, you see what I mean?"

Guy said: "Oh, right. Shit, that would be tough."

Buddy said: "No shit, Sherlock. I don't think you could do it."

Guy said: "You could do it though."

Buddy said: "Maybe. Just maybe. I mean, fuck. I think you may be onto something. I just don't know where to start."

Guy said: "Well, why don't we just limp on down to the welfare offices? See what happens. Oh, shit!"

The pizza was being ignored while they talked about welfare fraud. Some of the pepperoni was starting to blacken on the upturned edges. They both reached into the oven and grabbed a slice. Guy tried to hold his in his hand but it was too hot, even with the mitten/glove on. He put it on top of the stove. On the empty burner. The percolator taking up the other bottom burner. The frying pan taking up the upper-right one. The remaining burner was empty as well, but it didn't make sense for Guy to put his slice of pizza there. Because Buddy didn't have a burner to put his slice of pizza on, he transferred the slice of pizza back and forth in his hands, the right hand with the mitten/glove and the naked left hand. He was taking tiny little bites from it while he did this. Like a mouse. Just the edges. Guy's eyes were laser-focused on his slice of pizza. It wasn't steaming, or it was steaming, he couldn't see the steam though because of the heat coming from the oven. His eyes darted back and forth between his slice of pizza on the empty burner and what Buddy was doing with his slice. When Buddy finally was able to take a bite, an actual bite, from his slice of pizza, Guy picked up his slice of pizza from the empty burner and bit into the very tip of the triangle. It was good and nice and hot, but not too hot. Guy knew there were only two slices left after this one, so he did his best to savor the experience. The last slice would be almost bitter because it would be the end of things. But then again, he was the one that advocated for eating the pizza as quickly as possible. And in his mind, he was right. This was kind of torture. Just knowing that there was an end to things kind of made him miserable about it. Even though it was extremely tasty, what he was eating now. Guy would have preferred that this had ended before. To be done with the pizza. To move onto the crappy eggs and peanut butter and jelly sandwiches again. He was a "just end it all in a glorious go" kind of guy.

Whereas Buddy, who was really milking his pizza now, even though it wasn't too hot to eat anymore, he was taking small bites. Really getting as much out of it as he could. But, at the same time, relishing the idea that there was still one more slice. That this wasn't the end of it. That in the future they would, or he would, experience this again. And it really came down to the nature of their personalities. Buddy enjoyed a long slow burn of things, an almost tantric approach to living, where everything took as long as it took, and Guy, being the opposite, he mostly wanted to get all of the pleasure all at once and be done with it and move on. The pizza was the same as the masturbation, or how they viewed money, respectively. There was a huge overlap about it all, they both mostly wanted to be satisfied at all moments, however, when it came down to it, Buddy wanted to enjoy the long-form approach to things. The miniature bumps of good things, the minimal ditches of bad things, whereas Guy just wanted to get all the good, all at once, and then crash back down to Earth. And then, when he found himself in the gutter, he wanted to rebound right back up to the middle again. And who knows? Maybe they were both right? In a sense, Buddy was more realistic about things. He didn't get drawn into immediate machinations like Guy did. Where you get so upset about your finances that you run into your room crying and then the next minute you are rubbing one off because you suddenly got horny. On the other hand, though, Buddy was the kind of guy that would just stew in his own morass for no reason at all, thinking about a dead dog and not wanting to be alive anymore because he missed the dog. And really, the real tragedy of all of this, was that neither of their emotional proclivities mattered. Because the problem with these two was not their personalities, it was a problem with the system. And yes, Guy was right to think that the government should help them. What purpose is there for government if it isn't to help the neediest among us? But with regard to how to navigate the idea of what is available and capable of things that already exist, Buddy was way more pragmatic in his approach to eating pizza then Guy was. And because Guy was the kind of guy that would rather have everything all at once, his being, his thoughts, his way of thinking, were immediately thrown out the window in places like Wyoming, where everyone is supposed to be thrown in the grave the second they are born and then they have to drag themselves out of it just to get a single notion of what it feels like to be human. And whether Guy understood this implicitly or not, he did not, but he maybe did, he had some emotions about it, for certain, but he was not smart enough to actually do anything about it, and he mostly just felt his way along, like a mouse trying to get inside a building it knows food is in, but Buddy, Buddy somehow, merely because he was White and male and straight and American and on the edge of being middle-class, his mom was middle-class, his dad was not, but either way, growing up the way he did, he knew exactly what was required of him, so even though he had the same desires that Guy did, when he wanted to simply eat all the pizza slices with abandon, even though they both had different reasons for not doing the same thing, or not, because once Guy started eating his slice of pizza, he really started eating his slice of pizza, the difference was simple. In Buddy's mind, there was always going to be more pizza. Yes, maybe they only had one more slice of pizza now, but that didn't mean anything. There would be more pizza in the future. But with Guy, he didn't have that same thought. In his mind this was it. This was the last of the pizza. Once the pizza was gone, there would be no more pizza. And who knows, maybe never, there could quite possibly never be another pizza in the future. And yes, there was an overlap in their philosophies, but at the same time, Buddy was standing on a pillar, mentally, practically, philosophically, pragmatically, where he could easily and tantrically eat the pizza, because there was all the time in the world. Whereas with Guy, Guy didn't have that option. For Guy this pizza was the last pizza in the world. And it didn't matter how much he enjoyed it, there was no world, no just Society that would take pity on him for not having any more pizza to eat. And even though these two grew up with basically the exact same parents, in the exact same town, in the exact same Society, the way that Guy perceived the world versus the way Buddy perceived the world was vastly different. Guy not only didn't have the ability to relax when it came to eating food, he didn't have the luxury to relax when it came to eating food. And as much as this was a huge thing in Society, at the moment, when both Buddy and Guy were eating pizza, together, in a house without power or a way to pay the bills or rent, the different ways of eating pizza were not something large and global, like a testament on Society, it was something different entirely. Where Guy was the weirdo and Buddy was the good one.

> Buddy said: "Hey, man, slow down! You got to enjoy the good things in life! You can't just suck that shit down like a baby bird."
>
> Guy said: "What? I'm just eating my pizza."
>
> Buddy said: "Yeah, but you got to taste the flavors. The cheese and the pepperoni. I mean, you only live once, am I right? Just take a bite and go with it. Really take it in."
>
> Guy said: "It's pizza, man, I want to eat it."
>
> Buddy said: "Relax, there is going to be more, we aren't in any rush."
>
> Guy said: "Bullshit! We got this slice and then one more, then we're back to eggs and peanut butter. I'm hungry now."

Buddy said: "You don't know how to live."

Guy said: "I've lived. You eat pizza when you got pizza, what are you talking about?"

Buddy said: "I don't know, I just think you should enjoy things as they come."

Guy said: "This pizza was an accident, you're crazy, man. When? When are we going to get more pizza? For all we know the cops will show up tomorrow and kick us out of this place. I'm not going to sit around and have a good, like, lovefest with the slice of pizza I am eating, I mean, I want to eat it now! It's tasty and I like it."

Buddy said: "Yeah, you'll see."

Guy said: "See what? My pizza go away? It's going to do that anyway. What? Should I put the pizza in a safety deposit box or something? Let it, like, I don't know, appreciate in value? I mean, is that a thing? Can you just save everything for later? I mean, I grew up not sure if I would get beaten up in school because I was Mexican, do you think I should have just stayed home? Wait it out? I mean, what do you mean?"

Buddy said: "Bullshit, it wasn't that bad."

Guy said: "Oh! It was that bad, it is still that bad, you think you know, but you don't know."

Buddy said: "I don't remember school being that bad."

Guy said: "Dude, you are a White kid in a White school, in a White town, of course you don't remember it being that bad."

Buddy said: "Yeah, alright, my bad, but what does that have to do with pizza?"

Guy said: "Well, nothing, but you telling me to just relax and enjoy my pizza slice is a little much is all."

Buddy said: "I don't understand is all."

Guy said: "Yeah, I know!"

Buddy said: "I mean, but what can I do about it? It's not like I am the one making you feel bad about the pizza, right?"

Guy said: "No, you're right, but telling me to just enjoy the pizza, I mean, you're missing the point."

Buddy said: "Okay, then don't enjoy the pizza. What the fuck do I care?"

Guy said: "Well, leave me alone about it."

Buddy said: "Maybe I will."

Guy said: "Good, then do it."

Buddy said: "Done and done."

Guy said: "Well, good. Good job."

Buddy said: "Yeah, okay, good. But still..."

[14]

That "But still..." hung in the air like a moist stink. Guy was steeling himself. Trying not to become enraged. Buddy was trying his hardest to keep his mouth shut. He knew that if he could suspend his commentary for just a few moments, Guy would move on and not become enraged. But Buddy was having difficulty with this. He did not like to admit he was clueless about anything. Even though he was truly clueless about most things. He had an unquenchable desire to never be wrong. Even if it made him look like an asshole, or even hurt someone's feelings. He had always been like this. From a very young age. It was one of the main reasons he had trouble making friends. Why Guy was such a good friend, because he didn't care if he was right or wrong about anything. But, in this instance, when Buddy had had such a different upbringing to Guy's, a thing that Buddy couldn't actually fathom, which, in his uncreative way of thinking meant that it couldn't possibly be true that he didn't understand. Instinctively, Buddy understood he was not going to win this argument and that Guy, even though he seemed collected and unconcerned about Buddy's presumptions about how Guy should live his life and how he should view the world, Guy was quite upset. Upset enough that things could turn ugly pretty fast if he didn't let off. But still...Buddy was struggling to let it go. He knew he was right because everything in his body was telling him he was right. If he wasn't right, then his body would be telling him something different. He could prove it. He didn't know how, but he was sure he could. If he could enjoy the small pleasures in life, if things like eating a piece of pizza slowly was easy for Buddy, then it had to be easy for Guy as well. It was just a simple act of doing the thing. Like drinking a glass of water. You didn't have to chug water just because when you were growing up you didn't have very much water to drink, right? This argument sprung into Buddy's mind when he looked at the faucet. It proved he was right. There was no arguing that. But still...he was nervous to say it. Too nervous to say it. He was afraid the second he opened his mouth Guy would clock him. And he wasn't wrong. Guy was very close to clocking Buddy. Buddy was also a coward. A thing that he couldn't admit or even fathom. Ironically, had he been able to admit he was a coward, or fathom he was a coward, he could easily have seen Guy's point about the pizza. Because what made Buddy a coward had nothing to do with whether or not he was innately a coward. He was not. No human being is innately a coward. No one is born a coward. Even Buddy. It takes years and years of conditioning to become a coward. And sometimes cowards can become brave. And sometimes braves can become cowards. It all depends on the times and the circumstances and the ability to behave a certain way in certain situations. But what made Buddy a coward was the same thing that made him not understand where Guy was coming from with the pizza. Which was why he found himself unable to express his opinions at this very moment, the thing that led to this stand-off. Buddy's personality. Which was a thing repulsive to most people. A thing innate. Yes, Buddy may not have been born a coward, but he very much had been born annoying. His mom had noticed it very early on. He was a selfish child. A child unable to hear the word 'no.' The kind of child that would throw a tantrum at the tiniest perceived slight. Whether that was nap-time or not getting pizza for dinner. Buddy was the kind of kid that would show up to the basketball court with the only basketball, find his team losing, and instead of finishing the game, he would declare the ball was his and that he was going home. It was a tale as old as the Stranger myth. Buddy did not learn from adversity. He instead crept further and further into his own fiefdom. A place where he controlled everything. And the second anyone penetrated that space, Buddy would run away as fast as he could. Because staying there, either physically or mentally or emotionally, would require that he would have to see things from a different perspective than his own. And this scared him more than anything in the world. So, no, Buddy was not born a coward, but he turned himself into a coward as time went by. And the only thing keeping him from being absolutely terrified of Guy right now was the fact that his cowardice was somehow, just slightly, overshadowed by his desire to be correct. Because, for Buddy, his cowardice came second to his inborn annoyingness. Basically, because Buddy was born a dick, he was able to be a dick bravely. Even if it meant getting socked.

Guy watched Buddy thinking. The moist stink hanging in the air. The words "But still..." still ringing like church bells after the mallets have stopped. Guy was clenching and unclenching his mittened/gloved left hand. Buddy's looking like a typewriter with a single key stuck down. Guy was waiting for it to pop back up again. For Buddy to say something so offensive that he would have no choice but to react. They had wrestled earlier. But that was different. That was almost a friendly thing of frustration. This was serious. And it was serious for a simple reason. Guy, who had some very terrible baggage, naturally, from growing up un-White in a very racist place, the contract between he and Buddy, although unspoken, was an important contract: Buddy was not like Them. He was not one of Them. He was anti-Them, the same way that Guy was. And if Buddy were to cross that line, to turn Guy into the thing that he had felt his entire life growing up in Casper, where he didn't matter, because he was not White, that his identity was just something people tolerated, but refused to engage with, that from the moment Guy was born and until now, this very moment, he was expected to bend over backwards, as it were, to become more like "Them," and "They" were expected to do absolutely nothing to understand or even acknowledge that Guy was a human being with maybe a different understanding of life. Yes, if Buddy was to choose this path, to alienate his only true friend in the world over a thing that was truly trivial to Buddy, a thing that even Buddy himself understood was not in any way trivial to Guy, if Buddy chose to continue to ignore Guy's request to drop it, this thing would have very dire consequences to their relationship. Even if Guy didn't sock Buddy. Because it would be an act of betrayal on Buddy's side. And Buddy, who was the true dum-dum of the two, he understood one thing about it, that Guy was upset, but he did not understand why, he knew it was something more than normal, more important than normal, but he did not understand why, and Buddy, being the annoying dick that he was, continued to think of arguments to disprove Guy's clearly defined viewpoint on whether you were obligated to eat tasty pizza slowly when you only had a few slices left and life was not looking so hot for you at the moment.

Guy's big black eyes watched Buddy's tiny pinprick green eyes. Buddy was trying to find a way out of this stand-off without having his ego bruised. Or even less than that, of having his simple idea that life is the same for everyone because my life is the same as my life therefore your life is the same as my life. The wind kicked up outside the kitchen. The screen door still whacking against the building. This added to the tension. And the tension was idiotic. All that needed to happen was for Buddy to just give up. Admit he was wrong. Not even that. He didn't even need to do that. All he needed to do was drop it. Drop it and never bring it up again. Guy wasn't asking him to relitigate his past. To make a case for Wyoming Society. He didn't expect an apology from Buddy. All Guy wanted was for Buddy to simply just stop. And Buddy couldn't do it. He was incapable of doing it. He kept running the water analogy over and over again in his head. "You don't chug water because you grew up with very little water." Which wasn't even an argument. It was an indefensible statement. With no connection to reality. It was specious at best. A distraction from the actual issue, which was poverty. A thing that Buddy had never experienced. Even now, when they, meaning Guy and Buddy, were absolutely destitute, they were not impoverished. Sure, both of their moms would be quite annoyed if either of them moved back home, but they wouldn't say no. Especially if it was an emergency. Their current state of living was entirely of their own making. If anything, you could argue that Guy was still impoverished, in the sense that if it came down to it and they had to get more work, Guy was maybe more unlikely to find that prospect than Buddy because Guy was Mexican and Buddy was White. But that wasn't what was happening. But still...that would not prove Buddy's point either. And the one thing in the middle of the issue, the thing that made Buddy's point so grotesque, was that because he had not, in any way, ever, been lacking for anything growing up, or even now, even though they were living off of eggs and peanut butter and jelly in a house with no electricity, Buddy just could not wrap his head around the idea that anyone didn't have the exact same upbringing as he did. To the point where he just did not have the imagination to understand it. And the true tragedy of this moment was that Buddy, had he not been so dumb, he could have learned something, he could have expanded his understanding of the world, and he would have come away from it being a better human being. Instead, he took offense to being obtuse, to being un-omnipotent. And his ego couldn't stand it.

But still...even worse, really, was that Buddy and Guy were equal in a way. The issue was not the pizza, not really, the issue was the Society they lived in. And that Society was pitting the two friends against each other. And it was not Guy's responsibility to correct for this. It was Buddy's. But Buddy could never admit that. If you removed both of their upbringings and put them both where they were with no respect to how they got there, it was not a good thing that they were there. It was not either one of their faults. They were not lazy or stupid, sure, Buddy was a dum-dum and Guy was living in the clouds as they say, but so what? They had no problem working or going to work or having jobs, they just didn't want to have a horrible life, a horrible life that was only working and nothing else. Making tiny money for people that were only using them to make more money for themselves. It wasn't that complicated. And part of it too was the inability for either of these two to have a grand idea, a grand scheme of things about the future, which had nothing to do with anything, really, maybe if the schools they went to actually taught them things worth learning, like practical skills that would help them succeed in life, but it didn't work that way. Mostly because the school system in Wyoming was built in a way for kids to go to daycare so their parents could go to work. Which, surely that is something more to do with America than it has to do with Wyoming, but Wyoming surely did not figure out a better way to get children started out with skills, quite the opposite, if you are rich you go on to do rich things, everyone else has to do the actual work keeping Society functioning. So it was better for the kids to come out of high school with a horrible education, because it meant they would be forced to take the jobs that nobody wants to do, like washing dishes, or waiting tables, or digging ditches. And even though Guy and Buddy came from vastly different edges on the spectrum of growing up, when they finally met, after eighteen years in the system, plus some other years just living, it really didn't matter that Buddy had grown up needing nothing and Guy had grown up eating pizza really fast because he was poor. They were both equally fucked. And for them to even fight about what it meant to want for nothing and to want for anything was on purpose. And, in this instance, there is a possibility that Buddy was correct, that you should enjoy the things you have when you have them, but not because he was actually right. Guy and Buddy were in the same scenario, fighting each other on purpose as a distraction from the bigger thing that was hanging over their heads, a thing so big you couldn't even see it, or know it was there, it was so ubiquitous, that the class war was not between the poor and the middle class, but between the poor, the middle class, the upper middle class and the wealthy and the uber-wealthy.

Guy should not have had to defend himself. He understood this implicitly. Buddy, on the other hand, merely took his easy upbringing as proof that things were okay enough, and, therefore, nobody has it that bad. If I have enough, surely you have enough. And yes, we can relitigate this until the cows come home, Guy and Buddy could be working more, but they didn't. And it was not because they didn't desire to, or were even avoiding work, it was simply a function of: "What is the point?" They both loved money. They wanted more of it. All the time. But then you spend a few months stuck inside your home because the weather is so awful, maybe you miss a few days at work because of it, and then things kind of start to get out of hand. Then what? Life is hard and you don't really care that much because what is the point, so what? Only the truly ambitious can live in this world? The rest of us sleep in tents and eat eggs and peanut butter and jelly? Without a structure for Society that works for everyone, anyone that doesn't want to rule the world gets left behind. And Guy and Buddy got left behind. Buddy thought he might want to learn guitar one day, but because of the way things turned out, he could never even afford a guitar. Guy? Guy decided he was good at poetry, but he only managed to write down two lines in his young life. And those two lines were:

> I eat like a gun
> My hunger is a rifle

Guy and Buddy's lives were not free of ambition, they just didn't have a way to express themselves. They didn't not want to work, they were merely unsure what working even meant. Their parents had spent all of their childhoods working and it got them nowhere. And both Guy and Buddy had expected to get out into the real world with prospects and thoughts, after high school, but they were both very disappointed because aside from going to college and getting into a huge amount of debt for something neither of them were even slightly interested in, there was simply no choice. All of it, the market of work, was very dismal. You work fast food, or you work labor. Fast food was easier than labor but the pay was terrible.

However, we are here. And then what? The only option to get ahead in fast food is to work your way up, become the manager, buy a fast food restaurant for yourself, and then spend your life in fast food, or what? Guy and Buddy were basically trained to become something that kept the economy working without giving them anything to work towards. And it was depressing, and they were equals. Because of it. And Buddy should have just kept his mouth shut because Guy and Buddy were not enemies, they were simpatico, and even though Guy grew up poor and Buddy grew up middle class, they were in the same position, but Buddy, lacking any imagination, could not grasp this thought, and Guy, having lived the horrors of abject poverty, could not forget this simple idea, Buddy's. "But still..." was hanging like a wet fart in the kitchen. And Guy was having none of it.

[15]

"But still..." Buddy stood there looking like a stuck typewriter key. Guy stood there watching him. His left hand clenching and unclenching in the mitten/glove.

Guy said: "Just say it, man."

Buddy said: "Say what?"

Guy said: "What you're thinking."

Buddy said: "I'm not thinking anything."

Guy said: "Bullshit, man, you look like you got a turd in your butt, spit it out."

Buddy said: "I swear! I just look that way sometimes."

Guy said: "Bullshit, the fact that you didn't give me shit about what I said about having a turd in your butt proves it."

Buddy said: "How does that prove anything?"

Guy said: "Not saying nothing means you are thinking about something."

Buddy said: "You think I can't think of something and not say anything about it?"

Guy said: "I know you can't think something and not say nothing about it."

Buddy said: "You really think I am that stupid?"

Guy said: "Stupid or not, I just know you, it's not brain chemistry."

Buddy said: "Surgery."

Guy said: "See!"

Buddy said: "What?"

Guy said: "Don't act dumb, you know I just proved it. Out with it!"

Buddy had to admit that Guy was right. Or, he at least had to admit that Guy had a point. In his mind, Guy wasn't right at all, but now that things seemed to simmer down a little, mostly because Buddy couldn't hide his distraction, he decided to come clean.

Buddy said: "I can't!"

Guy said: "Why not?"

Buddy said: "Because I can't remember. Your stupid turd in your butt comment distracted me too much that I forgot what I was thinking and now I can't remember what I was thinking. I will say I was right though, whatever it was."

Guy said: "Likely story."

Buddy said: "It was good."

Guy said: "I am sure it was quite stupid."

Buddy said: "What is up with you today? You're kind of mean."

Guy said: "Why? 'Cause I called your idea stupid? You call me stupid all the time. How does it feel?"

Buddy said: "Well, it doesn't feel very good."

Guy said: "Welcome to my world."

Buddy said: "I still can't believe you have to eat your pizza that way, though."

Guy said: "Dude, I will punch you." Buddy looked at the sink.

Buddy said: "Water! It had something to do with water."

Guy said: "Man, just quit while you're ahead."

Buddy said: "No, but it was good! I proved it. You don't drink water like you eat pizza or something. Fuck! Why can't I remember? It's this fucking wind!"

Guy said: "Whatever."

Buddy said: "I'll remember, you'll see, and then you will be the idiot."

Guy said: "Well, I ain't holding my breath all day long."

Buddy said: "Well, you want to eat these last two slices?"

Guy said: "Nah, I'm tired."

Buddy said: "What? Are you going to take a nap or something?"

Guy said: "Nah, not that kind of tired. I just don't know. I don't think a nap would help."

Buddy said: "Well, that's depressing. Buck up, kid, things aren't too bad, ya know?"

Guy said: "And how is that? We have nothing. Worse than nothing. The pizza is almost gone, then what? What do we even have to look forward to? I'm sick of being broke and cold. I'm sick of Casper. I'm sick of Wyoming. I mean, I am sick of everything. I just want to sleep forever. Be done with it all."

Buddy said: "Well, let's make a plan to get out of here. It's not that bad, I mean, why don't we just get more shifts and, like, save some money or something? Move to Florida with my dad. At least there won't be any wind."

Guy said: "Yeah, but it's too late. We owe too much money. Getting more shifts won't help us because we will just have to pay back rent and back electricity. We will be here for years dealing with this."

Buddy said: "No, we just get more money and then not pay the rent and save it all, then we get like a bus ticket or something."

Guy said: "Yeah, but they will kick us out if we don't pay the rent and you can't work if you don't have a place to live."

Buddy said: "Well, what if we just lie to them and say the rent is in the mail for a couple months and then just ditch?"

Guy said: "Man, you are starting to sound like me. Have you turned into a goldfish or something? Didn't we already discuss this? It's too late. We could have done that months ago, but now it's too late. If we don't pay this month's rent the cops are going to come and kick us out, and then what? We move back home and save some money up? I mean, if I move back home, I mean, I don't even know what I would do. I think I may do something drastic."

Buddy said: "What do you mean? Like dark stuff?" This made Buddy a little sick to his stomach thinking Guy was so depressed he might kill himself.

Guy said: "Yeah, I don't know. I am not feeling very positive at the moment. And the idea of having my mom and dad giving me shit all day about what I am doing with my life, living in my old room, I mean, I already feel like a loser."

Buddy said: "Yeah, but you can't end it."

Buddy looked into Guy's big brown puppy dog eyes. He was indeed quite sad. Buddy hadn't seen him this sad before. He wondered if it had something to do with the pizza argument. But because Buddy was so self-obsessed, he couldn't connect how the pizza argument would change someone's mood this drastically. He lacked the imagination that was required to understand that yes, having to fight your best friend in the entire world about a very dear and closely held belief about the world, how having someone so close to you ignore the very essence of your being for the simple notion of being correct about something that was arbitrary to them, but was deeply rooted in yourself, how that sort of thing could mean the difference between feeling okay with the world and feeling totally alone in the world, how that could change your feelings about life, that life wasn't some long-standing reality that would persist forever, that really, life was a series of changing events that would define the next set of events, that maybe Buddy's insistence on Guy eating his pizza in a way that Buddy could agree with would make Guy feel isolated and alone, that a simple and acute rejection on a very simple and acute triviality, to Buddy, but not to Guy, could make Guy feel abandoned and sad, and Guy did feel abandoned and sad. He hadn't felt this alone since high school. Since being a teenager. Here, he and his best friend in the world were basically fighting for their lives and Buddy, his best friend in the world, was dismissing his feelings outright because he would rather win an argument than actually understand where Guy was coming from. Yes, Guy was sad. And yes, it only took that small thing to turn him from the very positive puppy that he had become in their very complicated and power-odd relationship, to a man on his own, wondering about what was going to happen next, and how what was going to happen next was not a positive thing. In fact, it was not a positive thing at all. It was a horrible thing there was no way out of. And yes, Guy, in general, was not the kind of person to just end it all on some whim, he didn't care. He kind of enjoyed life, things were mostly good and entertaining. He didn't spend very much time brooding about how horrible life was. He didn't really care one way or the other. Buddy did. Buddy was very dramatic when it came to his emotions. He didn't think about killing himself often, but the idea did come up sometimes. Especially when he was frustrated. But Buddy was too much of a coward to do it. Guy wasn't. Not that he wanted to do it, it was just, he would if it came down to it, because his entire existence was predicated on getting by. There was no secret complexity to Guy this way. He enjoyed being alive, but he didn't really enjoy suffering. He didn't have the same complex that Buddy had, where suffering was somehow proof that he was right and the world was wrong. Where his "woe is me" attitude actually kept him moving forward. Because as long as Buddy felt like a victim he could behave like a victim and nothing was his own fault. Whereas Guy, Guy took things at face value. He had spent an entire life being pushed down by Society. And because of this, there were exactly two options: Live, or Not Live. And the idea of going backwards, of going back home and living with his parents again, trying to get by, it just wasn't an option. Guy wasn't the kind of person that felt sorry for himself. He wasn't also a man of action, but when things came down to it, he would do what was necessary. And somehow Buddy understood this about Guy. Which is why it was almost shocking to hear the words coming out of his mouth that he would rather die than move back home. Which, after Buddy felt sick to his stomach when Guy said he would kill himself if he had to move back home, he, meaning Buddy, let that little bit of knowledge sink into his body. He became depressed himself. Almost matching the darkness that Guy was feeling. A certain hopelessness. And for the first time in Buddy's life, he actually felt the emotions somebody else around him was having.

He said: "Well, what do we do then?"

Guy said: "I don't know. There doesn't seem to be too many options."

Buddy said: "Yeah, but if you bite it, I don't think I would be able to stick around myself."

Guy said: "You'd be fine. You could just move to Florida or something. I mean, you wouldn't mind moving back home for a while. I mean, you'd probably annoy your mom so bad she would buy you a bus ticket. Maybe even give you some money to keep you from coming back."

Buddy said: "Yeah, maybe. She would be quite pissed if I moved back in, that is for sure. But, c'mon! Things aren't that bleak, man!"

Guy said: "I don't know, man, we are fucked pretty hardcore here. We really got nothing. I mean, what? We pay a little rent and hope they don't kick us out, and then pay some electric bill stuff and hope we get heat again? And then we just work all year to pay old bills and keep living like this? No way out, just barely getting by? I mean, I don't mean to be dark about it, but somehow eating that pizza just really put things into perspective for me, I don't know if I can do this anymore. I mean, I want to go take a nap, but the bedroom is so cold. I don't even know if I can sleep there tonight. I may just come in here and sleep on the linoleum. And then what? Tomorrow is the exact same? The wind still blowing, the bills still waiting, the cops showing up to kick us out? Then what? Sleeping in the gutter, or going back home, I mean, if I go back to my mom's, I can't even get to work anymore. Then what? I get a job as a paperboy. Dust my BMX off in the garage? I mean, I can't live like a loser anymore. I'm done with it. It's too much, I can't take it!"

Buddy said: "Well, what if we borrowed some money?"

Guy said: "Dude! You are a goldfish. We have been through this already. Our options are nothing and nil. It's too damn late! We missed our chance. Had we been smarter we would have thought this up months ago. Instead we now got nothing."

Buddy said: "Well, if you would have just mailed those electric bills."

Guy said: "I did! I swear I did!"

Buddy said: "Obviously you didn't."

Guy said: "It doesn't matter, because it is too late now anyway."

Buddy said: "Well, you should have mailed them."

Guy said: "And you should have paid the rent."

Buddy said: "Yeah, but you never paid me rent money."

Guy said: "You never asked!"

Buddy said: "You don't think the rent needs to be paid every month? I shouldn't have to ask."

Guy said: "Bullshit! You didn't ask because you didn't want to pay it."

Buddy said: "Yeah, but you should have noticed we weren't paying rent."

Guy said: "Oh, you can't put that on me!"

Buddy said: "Well, where did the money go, Guy?"

Guy said: "I don't know, you know I have problems with money, where did your money go, Buddy?"

Buddy said: "I don't know, maybe you stole it from my stash. To, I don't know, buy candy or something?"

Guy said: "Yeah, I stole all your rent money to buy candy, real mature."

Buddy said: "Yeah, well."

Guy said: "'Yeah, well' is right. We're fucked and you know it."

Buddy said: "Yeah, but."

Guy said: "Admit it."

Buddy said: "Admit what?"

Guy said: "That we're fucked."

Buddy said: "We're not fucked."

Guy said: "Dude, we're fucked. There are zero options. We're fucked."

Buddy said: "We're not that fucked. We got options."

Guy said: "Yeah? Sock 'em to me."

Buddy said: "What?"

Guy said: "Sock me the options."

Buddy said: "You can't sock somebody options."

Guy said: "You know what I mean."

Buddy said: "There are options. Just let me think a minute."

Guy said: "Just admit it, man."

Buddy said: "I won't! I refuse."

Guy said: "We're fucked. Just say it."

Buddy said: "I won't."

Guy said: "You have to!"

Buddy said: "Why? For what reason?"

Guy said: "Because the sooner you admit it, the sooner we can figure out what to do."

Buddy said: "Yeah, but I don't believe it."

Guy said: "We're fucked."

Buddy said: "We're not fucked."

Guy said: "You're not making an argument otherwise."

Buddy said: "I don't need to. Things are fine."

Guy said: "How are things fine? We're fucked."

Buddy said: "Even if we are fucked, what the hell do you want to do about it?"

Guy said: "I don't know, decide, I guess."

Buddy said: "Decide about what?"

Guy said: "I don't know, the future."

Buddy said: "What's what though? How is there even anything to decide about?"

Guy said: "Oh, I don't know, the future of things."

Buddy said: "What are you even saying?"

Guy said: "I don't know, it's pretty clear what we should do here."

Buddy said: "Nooooo!"

Guy said: "Yes."

Buddy said: "We can't. That is too depressing. C'mon, how would that even work?"

Guy said: "I don't know, but it is better to end things on our own terms than waiting around for all the bullshit to collapse."

Buddy said: "Yeah, but..."

Guy said: "Yeah, but really. All we have to do is just decide and that will be that. It will all be over and we can stop worrying."

Buddy said: "Yeah, but, we don't even have, like, guns or knives or nothing. What are we going to do? Go outside and get killed by the wind? It's cold, but it's not that cold. Winter is over, man."

Guy said: "Well, we could hang ourselves. With, like, our belts or something."

Buddy said: "What belts? I don't have a belt. Do you have a belt?"

Guy said: "I think so, I got that braided leather thing."

Buddy said: "Okay, so you hang yourself with your belt and then what? I take you down and do myself?"

Guy said: "Yeah, I don't know. I guess."

Buddy said: "And how would that work? You can't tie a belt to anything, you wouldn't have any room for your neck. Belts are kind of short, I think."

Guy said: "Well, what if we ran a bath and drowned ourselves?"

Buddy said: "Same problem. What? I drown and then you take me out and drown yourself? I mean, you would have to hold me down. Who is going to hold you down?"

Guy said: "I don't know, maybe I could find some bricks or something?"

Buddy said: "That's stupid."

Guy said: "See! See how you call me stupid all the time?"

Buddy said: "I didn't mean it. I just meant your idea was stupid."

Guy said: "It's the same thing!"

Buddy said: "It's not! A stupid idea is not the same as calling someone stupid."

Guy said: "By association it is!"

Buddy said: "Well, sorry for living, but how the hell are you going to put bricks on your back while you kill yourself? It seems kind of impossible. To me. Sorry for bringing it up."

Guy said: "Well, what's your big idea then? You got no good ones that I am hearing."

Buddy said: "Yeah, I don't, because I don't think we should do it." Guy looked at the percolator and had a moment of brilliance.

Guy said: "What about that?"

Buddy said: "What's that?"

Guy said: "The Bubbler."

Buddy said: "What do you mean?"

Guy said: "I mean, what if we just put that thing on full-blast and let it blow us to smithereens with the lid on?"

Buddy took a moment to let this idea fester. Guy was right. If they put the thing on "full-blast," as he had called it, with the lid on, the thing would explode the entire apartment with the best friends in the world still inside. They would feel nothing. Maybe just a short burst of hot air, and then, Whammo! They would be free of this world. Buddy didn't like the idea of dying, but as far as ways to die, this was a stroke of genius on Guy's part. Buddy took a moment to respond.

Guy became impatient and said: "Well, what do you think?"

Buddy said: "You know, Guy, you might be a genius after all."

[16]

The mood in the apartment shifted immediately. Their money problems solved. Not just their money problems, but all of their problems. And it was Guy's genius idea that had done it. Buddy was impressed with Guy's sudden prowess. He said as much, he said: "Damn, Guy, you are on a hot streak today! Mystery pizza, winning arguments, and now this. I mean, this may be the best day of your life. You should be proud." Guy was not thinking that. He was still processing the idea of getting blown up to avoid paying the bills. But now that Buddy had put it that way, he was proud of himself. It was a good day for him. He said as much, he said: "Well, if you put it that way, it is a good day for ol' Guy! Too bad there isn't a way to celebrate." Buddy thought about this. About the future and their plans. He patted the wad of money in his pocket. He tried to take it out, but the mitten/glove got in the way. He took it off and put the money on the counter. He started to put his mitten/glove back on. As he was doing this, Guy took his mitten/glove off and asked Buddy to hold it. Guy picked up the money like he was going to count it. He started to pretend to count it while keeping an unknown eye on Buddy. Buddy absentmindedly put the left mitten/glove on his left hand. Guy found it very hard to hide his very large smile from Buddy, but he managed to. His face was aimed towards the floor like he was looking at the money. When he straightened it his face was neutral again. He put the money on the counter and said: "Damn! That's a lot of dough!" He may have just tricked Buddy into taking his mitten/glove, but the reason Buddy had taken the money out of his pocket was completely lost to him.

Buddy said: "No, you dum-dum, we can spend it now!"

Guy said: "What do you mean?"

Buddy said: "What do you mean, what do I mean? We are free and clear, dog! That money is ours."

Guy said: "Well, not yet though. We have to die first."

Buddy said: "Man, I thought you were a genius today. We can't spend it if we're dead, and not only that, but it will blow up with us. What, do you think our ghosts will come back down to Earth and need some walking around money? I guess, floating around money, I should say."

Guy said: "Yeah, but if we spend it before we're dead isn't that like stealing? Won't god get mad at us for that?"

Buddy said: "For spending our own hard-earned cash? I don't think god works that way."

Guy said: "Yeah, but it doesn't belong to us."

Buddy said: "It doesn't not belong to us. It's ours until we spend it. Then it is someone else's."

Guy said: "Even if we owe money?"

Buddy said: "Even if we owe money."

Guy said: "But maybe we should, like, bury it under a rock or something for the landlord. Like leave a note."

Buddy said: "Are you joking?"

Guy said: "Not really, I feel bad that we owe money. I just feel like it might be a nice gesture, is all."

Buddy said: "As nice of a gesture as blowing up the landlord's apartment on our way out?"

Guy said: "I mean, if you put it that way."

Buddy said: "I am putting it that way."

Guy said: "Well, what did you have in mind?"

Buddy said: "I don't know, maybe we party down one last time. Buy some beer and smokes, get rip roaring drunk and go out in a blaze of drunkenness. We can buy some nudie mags, have one last glorious wank, I mean, we could buy anything."

Guy said: "Like a car? Drive to Florida?"

Buddy said: "It's not that much money."

Guy said: "A bus ticket to Florida?"

Buddy said: "Then what?"

Guy said: "I don't know, then we can live in Florida."

Buddy said: "I don't want to move to Florida. You're depressing me, man, maybe we should just fire the thing up now and get it over with."

Guy said: "No, I'm not ready."

Buddy said: "Okay, then think up something good you want for your last day on Earth. Mind you it needs to be nearby, preferably at the gas station."

Guy thought about this for a while. Buddy was bemused watching him think. He warmed his hands with the open stove. He looked at his hands. How the hell was he wearing two mittens/gloves again? Guy really was becoming a genius. Buddy started to rethink the suicide pact they had made. Not because it was a bad idea, but because Guy was on such a roll, maybe he belonged in the world for a longer amount of time.

Guy said: "Well, beer, yes, that is good, and smokes, and nudie mags, all good things. But also, I think we should get some candy bars and chips and chocolate milk. And maybe that pair of sunglasses I have been wanting for like ever. I wish gambling was legal here, like Montana, I mean, we could spend the rest on scratch tickets and maybe get lucky enough to not have to blow ourselves to bits."

Buddy said: "Yeah, right? For such a "freedoms" kind of place to live, they sure don't want you to do shit like that. Why is that?"

Guy said: "I have no clue. Jesus?"

Buddy said: "Yeah, prolly. Either that, or all the freedoms are a bunch of bullshit."

Guy said: "Okay! Should we go? No time like the present to get fucked up!" Just then a huge gust of wind blew in. Rattled the back of the apartment building. The windows shook. The screen door was whacking like crazy.

Buddy said: "Fucking wind. That kinks our plans. Why don't you go out and get the supplies and I will wait for you, make sure the apartment doesn't blow away?"

Guy said: "How about you go, and I will keep the stove burning so it's nice and warm when you get back?"

Buddy said: "I don't want to go out there."

Guy said: "C'mon, we gotta try!"

Guy grabbed the money from the counter and put it in his pocket. This made Buddy nervous. But then he was able to let his nervousness slide because in a few hours it wouldn't matter anyway whether or not Guy had all of their money in his pocket. Plus, it's not like he was going anywhere that Buddy wasn't going. He could keep an eye on him. They walked to the front door. Guy looked at Buddy. Buddy looked at Guy.

Guy said: "You ready?"

Buddy got serious and nodded. Guy turned the knob. The wind pushed the door open, and Guy let go. The knob went into the hole it had made earlier in the wall. Both of their stocking caps blew off. Guy started to push himself outside. The wind was too intense. He got onto the porch and had to hold onto the railing. Somehow the money hadn't made it all the way into his pocket. The wad got sucked out and flew back into the apartment. Both Buddy and Guy turned towards the inside. A look of shock on both of their faces. The money exploded into a flurry of bills, some of them landing in the oven. They could see it from the porch. Buddy ran back to the kitchen and managed to grab the bills before they caught on fire. Guy wrestled the door closed before any of the bills flew out into the world. The closing of the door created a gush of wind that sent the bills into a second flurry. More bills went into the oven. Buddy managed to save them before they caught on fire. One of the bills slipped through the oven rack. Buddy burned his hand getting this one out. But only barely. Luckily, he was wearing the mittens/gloves. Guy and Buddy went around the apartment collecting the money. When they thought they had it all, Guy said: "All there?" Buddy counted it.

Buddy said: "I guess, I can't remember how much we had. But this seems right."

Guy said: "What the fuck was that? Man, this wind should be illegal."

Buddy said: "Right? They can ban gambling, but they let the wind blow like this? It ain't right."

Guy said: "Well, shit. What now?"

Buddy said: "I don't know. The wind really puts a kink in things."

Guy said: "Well, maybe we can do a pizza thing, but with beer and smokes. They deliver that stuff?"

Buddy said: "Not that I know of."

Guy said: "They should do that. It would be a good business."

Buddy said: "It's probably illegal."

Guy said: "Yeah, but you can buy drinks at the drive-through bar places. How can that be legal, but not delivering the stuff?"

Buddy said: "I don't know, Wyoming is stupid. Haven't you noticed? It's all a bunch of lies."

Guy said: "Yeah, I noticed. Maybe we could get the cops to drop something off? The cops will show up for anything."

Buddy said: "Yeah, but they show up because you are doing stuff like getting beer and smokes. Or gambling. Not because you need beer and smokes or some scratch cards. However, you're Mexican, maybe I can call them and tell them a Mexican came to my house and he needs to leave, but I don't have any beer and smokes to make him look like he is drunk. And then they will bring beer and smokes and maybe even drugs to plant on you?"

Guy said: "Then what? I go to jail and you get drunk and smoke on your own?"

Buddy said: "Works for me!"

Guy said: "You're a dick. You would do that wouldn't you?"

Buddy said: "For beer and smokes? In a heartbeat. And if they gave me the drugs too, I would tell them you also raped the dog."

Guy said: "We don't have a dog."

Buddy said: "Not anymore, it ran away after you raped it."

Guy said: "Some friend you are."

Buddy said: "Don't blame me, you're the Mexican in Wyoming."

Guy said: "Yeah, but I'm half-Italian."

Buddy said: "Try telling the cops that, Rape-Boy."

Guy said: "I know you are joking, but you understand that is true."

Buddy got serious. Because it was true. Buddy could call the cops on Guy and tell them anything he wanted and they would believe him and Guy would go to jail. The only way that Guy could get out of it was if there was a Black man there too that Guy could blame for whatever it was that Buddy accused Guy of doing. Then they would both go to jail, but Guy would get released and the Black guy would have to spend the night in jail.

Buddy said: "Yeah, I know. I'm sorry. But still, you shouldn't rape our dog, you pervert."

Guy said: "You know who likes it doggy style?"

Buddy said: "Let me guess, my mom?"

Guy said: "Nope, your sisters! Your mom likes anal!"

Buddy said: "Whatever, lettuce dick."

Guy said: "Whatever, I put it in your mom and a broccoli came out."

Buddy said: "That's genital warts, my friend."

Guy said: "Dude, you just said your mom has warts!"

Buddy said: "Nuh-uh, I was saying you thought your dick was broccoli, but it was warts instead."

Guy said: "So I gave your mom warts?"

Buddy said: "No, you have warts, you didn't give my mom anything."

Guy said: "But a good time? Butt a good time. See what I did there?"

Buddy said: "Very clever." Guy got sad. He liked these conversations with Buddy. They were fun and usually entertaining. As long as Buddy didn't go too far and could understand where the lines were drawn.

Guy said: "I am going to miss this."

Buddy said: "What? Talking about warts?"

Guy said: "Yeah, no. Maybe? I mean, yes, I like hanging out with you."

Buddy said: "Don't go soft on me now."

Guy said: "I'm serious. What if we aren't together after this thing happens? I don't want to be alone again."

Buddy said: "It won't matter, man. It's the great big beyond, who the hell knows what's out there? If it's anything like this place, we will be together for like infinity. I mean, the way I see it, if we croak together, we will stay together."

Guy said: "If that is true, we should hold onto the money as well, right? Just in case."

Buddy said: "Good point."

Buddy took the money from the counter where he had placed it after counting it. He folded it. Put it in his pocket. He wondered if he would have pants in the afterlife. They stood there in the kitchen. Not knowing what to say to each other. They both had a pit in their stomach about dying. Scared, but resigned. The thought was too abstract to comprehend. Both of them believed in god, in something after the life they were living, but it wasn't really anything concrete. Guy was Catholic, so his ideas were more codified than Buddy's were, but they were still vague. Guy thought he would meet Jesus and god and Saint Peter and there would be clouds and old relatives. Buddy, who had grown up almost without any religion, a few times in his life he had gone to church, and it was always boring and stupid, he thought that maybe god would come around and explain some stuff to him, and then he would just kind of cruise around the universe for a while. Maybe even come back to Earth at some point. It all seemed kind of fun, in some way. Like being dead just meant you could watch people shower without their knowledge. He didn't really have anything more complicated in mind. But he did assume there was a god because why else would things suck so bad? Or why would he be so right about everything? Buddy's belief in god was more of a belief in himself than anything else. And since he couldn't imagine himself being anywhere but here, and now, and true and pure, and right, always right, how could the afterlife be any different? And as much as he did not like the idea of someone else being in control of things, he very much liked the excuse that nothing was his fault. God, to him, was just something else to blame for his shortcomings. And Buddy, the narcissist that he was, assumed that he and god would have a nice long sit-down when he died. And Buddy would tell god all the things god had fucked up about life. And then, of course, god would acquiesce and apologize for not giving Buddy the life he deserved. And, at that point, god would send Buddy back to Earth to rule the planet with all of his great ideas. Buddy was certain of this. And Buddy was afraid to die. He didn't want to die. But he could see a good outcome from it. And that was enough for him to continue with their plan. Guy, on the other hand, was a little nervous. He had always been taught that suicide was sinful. In his mind it was okay, not suicide, but dying, as long as Buddy was the one that did the thing. Guy would have to be a bystander is all. An accident. And that is how he left it.

[17]

There wasn't much for Guy and Buddy to do anymore on Earth. It was too windy to go get party favors for their last day on Earth. It was too cold everywhere else in the apartment, so they stood in the kitchen. In front of the oven. Buddy wearing Guy's mittens/gloves. Warming his hands on the heat coming from the oven. Guy's hands were bare. Happy to have tricked Buddy into taking the mittens/gloves.

Guy said: "Now what?"

Buddy said: "I don't know, we could eat the last two slices of pizza."

He put the pizza into the oven. They stood there looking. Watching it heat up.

Buddy said: "So, are you going to go whack it one more time? You know, before the kablooey."

Guy said: "Yeah, no. Not really in the mood."

Buddy said: "Well, that's sad. I mean, I give you permission to think about my mom. Just this once though."

Guy said: "Yeah, no. It just doesn't feel right. I mean, you can't just whack one before getting up to the pearly gates, you know? That seems weird. Especially if I think about your mom while I do it. Probably send me to hell for that alone."

Buddy said: "Man, your religion stuff is weird."

Guy said: "What do you mean? Doesn't your religion have something against whacking off?"

Buddy said: "I don't know, prolly, I mean, not like yours, it's not like a dreadful sin or whatever you call it."

Guy said: "Deadly sin. I don't think whacking off is a deadly sin though."

Buddy said: "Isn't it like lust or something?"

Guy said: "Yeah, maybe. I don't know. It just doesn't feel right is all."

Buddy said: "Yeah, I hear ya. I don't feel like it either. I mean, I don't think I could even concentrate at the moment."

Guy said: "Freaked out?"

Buddy said: "A little, you?"

Guy said: "Very much."

Buddy said: "The pizza looks done."

They reached into the oven and each grabbed their last slice. Buddy was doing his normal savoring, taking little bites and enjoying each one. Guy was doing the same this time.

Buddy said: "Hey! Look at you, enjoying the little things in life."

Guy said: "I hate to tell you that is not what is happening. I just can't eat. My stomach hurts. I'm scared, Buddy. I don't want to die."

Buddy said: "Neither do I, but what else are we going to do? I mean, tomorrow the cops might show up and kick us out. We got no money, no way to get any money. The wind won't stop blowing and life just really sucks, man."

Guy said: "Yeah, I guess."

Buddy said: "You got any better ideas? Mystery pizza-style?"

Guy said: "No, it just feels weird to give up hope is all. I mean, to just end it all instead of trying more."

Buddy said: "Nah, it'll be fine. Like taking a nap. A big ol' kabloom of a nap. And then we will be in a better place."

Guy said: "Yeah, I don't know. I guess."

Buddy said: "You'll see, we will meet on the other side and have a great big laugh about it. They'll have food for us, and rent will be free, and there will be naked ladies waiting for hunks like us to pass over. I mean, it's going to be a blast."

Guy said: "You don't sound so convinced." Buddy wasn't convinced. He was trying to convince himself by convincing Guy.

Buddy said: "Yeah, I just don't know what else to do. I'm trying to stay positive here."

Guy said: "Well, alright. I trust you. I mean, let's get it over with, before I lose my nerve."

Buddy said: "You sure?"

Guy said: "No, are you?"

Buddy said: "No."

They stood there eating the pizza. Slowly. So slowly that Guy stopped eating it altogether. He put his slice back into the box. His big puppy dog brown eyes looking sad. Buddy couldn't look at him. It was too painful. He continued to eat his pizza. Not thinking about it. There was no taste. Just different textures in his mouth. He couldn't believe things had come this far. That they were actually going to do it. They were actually going to blow themselves up instead of finding a way to pay the rent and bills. But as hard as Buddy tried, he couldn't think of anything else to do. Guy as well. Guy wasn't even thinking about how to solve the problems anymore, he was simply, pragmatically, going about the last motions of his short and pitiful life. Just going along. Like always. Buddy too, for that matter. But Buddy was still a little bit hopeful that something would come up. Some new miracle would present itself when the stress of almost dying really kicked in. Like some unseen force changing everything. Like the miracle pizza. The mystery pizza. Because that was always the way with Guy and Buddy, they were a good team, even though they got themselves into more trouble by being together, they always managed to solve their problems together in a miraculous and mysterious way. Each of them alone would never make it in the world, but together, they stood a chance. But it really did seem like their luck had finally run out. There would be no miracle coming. No mysterious knock on the door. No salvation. They were finally and totally on their own. They couldn't deny that any longer. And the darkness was starting to feed back on the darkness. An echo chamber of inertia. Where the blackness became blacker with each round. Both self-propagating and self-actuating at the exact same time. There was only one way this could end, and it was the worst possible ending. For them. The snake of hope was eating its own tail. Soon there would be nothing but an empty black void where life used to be. And the more Guy and Buddy spent time in this feedback loop of hopeless inertia, the more they got used to it. It was the same emotion soldiers get in battle, the same emotion from a fascist takeover of Society, where death is not only a simple outcome, but the most likely outcome, and because death feeds upon death, death is the only thing that makes sense anymore. A place where only the rigid and most disciplined among the living could even stand a chance at survival. Those hyper-focused and self-serving individuals among us. Who, against every single odd, had a desire to survive that was larger than the destruction ubiquitous. Guy and Buddy did not have this thing. The thing humans needed to survive trench warfare, or even the Holocaust. Guy and Buddy would be the first to get shot, the first to be rounded up and taken to the camps. And then they would be gone, and nobody would even notice they were gone. They knew this. Instinctively.

Both Guy and Buddy were sad about a similar thing. Their moms. Of all the people in the world that would miss them, it was their moms. But a very ironic twist to this sadness they felt about leaving this world, while leaving their moms behind to miss them, was that both of their moms were at the center of them deciding to end things this way. Had their moms made them feel like it was okay to come home, to ask for help, to get help from them, they would have easily gone home and asked for help. As it was, the nature of their relationships with their moms caused them to write their moms off. And while Guy and Buddy were not blaming their moms for having arrived at this simple conclusion, they did hold them a little responsible for this. Whether it was valid reasoning or not. Guy and Buddy were still quite young. They hadn't been away from home long enough to understand that you need to take control of your own life and there is almost no help when you find yourself truly independent. And as such, in both of their minds, their moms were to blame for the darkness they were experiencing. However, there was almost exactly nothing either of their moms could have done to stave off this dramatic turn of events, short of giving them money. Whether this was an indictment of their moms is up for debate. Buddy was an annoying child that grew into an annoying adult. Guy was a listless spaced out child that grew into a listless spaced out adult. These were things that were innate for Guy and Buddy. From birth. They hadn't changed, either of them, since being toddlers. And you can't polish things that are things all the way through themselves. What was wrong or right with Guy and Buddy was wrong or right from day one. And sure, they could have tried harder, they could have tried to get better, or gone to college, or worked more, but it was never going to happen. They knew it, meaning the moms, and Guy and Buddy knew it. It wasn't some huge surprise that Guy and Buddy turned out the way that they did. And even if it was maybe disappointing to their moms, they had given up trying to change them about the exact same time in life. Meaning, the second these two became teenagers, it was all over. And that was it. For over a decade the moms had watched both of these boys turn into men who were the exact same thing as they were when they turned thirteen. And much like the echo-chamber feedback loop of inertia that Guy and Buddy were experiencing, their moms had been experiencing the same thing with respect to them for over a decade. Which meant, really, that yes, their moms would be sad when they blew themselves up in order to not pay rent or bills, but it would not come as a surprise. And they would mourn them, like all moms mourn their children, but later in their lives, when they thought back to both Guy and Buddy growing up, they would both shake their heads. Because at some point, nothing really changes. So, no, Guy's and Buddy's moms were not to blame for what was happening at this exact moment. Not in the least. They had tried their hardest to get these two on the right track. And the right track did not agree with the direction Guy and Buddy were heading the moment they started growing pubic hair and started spending long hours in the shower, doing who the hell knows what. Because no mom wants that question answered. It is best to not think about it.

Buddy started getting the percolator ready. The Bubbler, as they called it. He emptied out the used coffee from the tuna can with holes connected to the tube. He rinsed the thing. He rinsed the carafe. He filled it with water. Put it on the counter. He put the tuna can with holes connected to the tube into the water. He put new coffee grounds into the tuna can with holes. He put the lid with holes on top of that. He then did the thing that was going to end both him and Guy, he put the top lid on. This was a dark moment for both Guy and Buddy. Guy was watching Buddy do this. He didn't want to touch the apparatus. For religious reasons. But he was quite aware of what was happening. They both let out a sigh, a despondent sigh, when Buddy put the lid with the glass thing on. It was simple. They were sealing their fate with that one motion. Buddy put the Bubbler, the percolator, on the stove. He looked at Guy, who had gone around to the other side of the open oven door to allow Buddy to make the bomb. Guy nodded at Buddy. Buddy turned the gas on. Full blast, like they had talked about.

> Guy said: "Hey, why don't we do it on like low? I mean, maybe we should give ourselves a little time, ya know?"
>
> Buddy said: "But it won't work though."
>
> Guy said: "But it will though, right? It's not about the thing getting hot real fast, it is the thing about it getting to the point of, like, I don't know, explosion, right? It doesn't matter how it gets there, it just needs to get there, right?"
>
> Buddy said: "I don't know, I'm not a science guy, like a, I don't know, you know what I mean!"

Guy said: "But it's like you said. The bubbles crawl up the edges and stuff, right? It doesn't matter how long it takes, it's just they need to get there, right?"

Buddy had no idea. And Guy calling him out on his bullshit only made Buddy double-down.

Buddy said: "Oh, right, right! You're right. That will buy us some time. Give us some time to think. Good call." Buddy turned the knob to low. This action changed the mood. Things went from being very intense to being slow and boring. Instead of intense heat building up to a great big explosion, there was a slow burn that would eventually get them to where they wanted to go. Buddy said: "You sure this is the way to go?"

Guy said: "It doesn't matter either way, we will get there eventually. At least now we can spend our last few moments on Earth relaxed, right? Instead of freaked out. I mean, I don't know, I kind of want to enjoy our last moments."

Buddy said: "Haha! Really? You want to take it slow, really take it in?"

Guy said: "What do you mean?"

Buddy said: "Well, I mean, your pizza thing, now suddenly you want to do it real slow?"

Guy said: "This has nothing to do with pizza, man! I'm just not ready to go kablam. How is that so hard to understand?"

Buddy said: "I'm not saying that you want to, like, have tantric sex with blowing ourselves to bits, I just mean, how is this different than eating pizza?"

Guy said: "Eating pizza is different than getting dead, man."

Buddy said: "How? Tell me. What the hell do you care? There is nothing happening in these next few minutes that is going to change anything. It's not like we are savoring some good great times. I mean, we can't even get outside to buy smokes and beer. What is there to hold onto? At least with pizza you can have some good flavors, right?"

Guy said: "Yeah, but dropping dead is not like eating pizza, when you drop dead, that is it, with pizza you get like another slice or whatever."

Buddy said: "Do you though? There is no new slice for sure. Certain even. You know what I mean? I mean, it is uncertain. That is what I mean."

Guy said: "Yeah, but why the big rush? I say, let it ride, give us a few moments to sort things out, is all."

Buddy said: "Yeah, okay, I don't disagree, I just want you to notice that you are going against your whole 'I only eat pizza fast' kind of thing. Because you don't."

Guy said: "But I do! It's just with pizza I have reasons, with getting blown up, what the hell do I know? What the hell do you know?"

Buddy said: "I don't know, but you giving me shit about giving you shit about eating pizza seems a little rude in comparison."

Guy said: "I wasn't giving you shit, I just wanted you to know that giving me shit was bullshit, is all."

Buddy said: "What? Because growing up was hard for you and now you want to feel okay about it? What do I know about that sort of shit?"

Guy said: "I don't know, trust me, maybe? Be cool with my emotions for once? What the hell do you care? It's not like I need you to live your life the same way as me, right? I mean, I could care less if you, I don't know, wiped your ass from your butthole to your balls, right? Why fuck with me about pizza?"

Buddy said: "Because it is the same thing! Like drinking water. You don't drink water like a maniac because you grew up not having water, right?"

Guy said: "What? That argument is stupid, what do I care about water?"

Buddy said: "Yeah, but you had lots of water growing up."

Guy said: "Yeah, and?"

Buddy said: "Well, I mean, it's like pizza."

Guy said: "Oh! Now I see, this was the thing you wouldn't say earlier."

Buddy said: "Yeah, no, what do you mean?!"

Guy said: "When you were like 'But, still...,' this is what you were talking about. That somehow water is your proof."

Buddy said: "Yeah, well, no, but maybe."

Guy said: "Dude, having a few extra moments of life is different than eating pizza. You think I am the dum-dum, you are the dum-dum."

Buddy said: "Yeah, you'll see. It will all be shown to both of us soon enough."

Guy said: "Bullshit! Admit it, man! Eating pizza is different than getting blown up by the Bubbler."

Buddy said: "Yeah, but only slightly."

Guy said: "So you admit it!"

Buddy said: "No! Don't put words in my mouth!"

Guy said: "We'll see. Soon enough."

Buddy said: "Same to ya. I'm not wrong, ya know, you gotta just roll with the punches."

Guy said: "It's not punches when everything is Society strangling you, man."

Buddy said: "Yeah, but it's not as bad as you think is all I am saying."

Guy said: "For you, maybe."

Buddy said: "Yeah, but we are in the same boat!"

Guy said: "For now."

Just then. At this very moment when both Guy and Buddy were intensely arguing with each other. Thinking that life was about to be over. That the percolator was about to explode, sending them both into the ether. Both of them terrified of death. Not truly committed to dying just to save themselves from having to pay their bills. The percolator started percolating. And it kept percolating. It did not explode. The clear water slowly turned brown, then it turned black. Guy and Buddy didn't know what to do with this information.

Guy said: "Shit."

Buddy said: "Uh, right?"

Guy said: "What does that mean?"

Buddy said: "I guess we don't get blown to smithereens."

Guy said: "Thank-fucking-god!"

Buddy said: "Yeah, right?"

Guy said: "What now?"

Buddy said: "I don't know. I guess we just wait till tomorrow and go pay some rent and hopefully they don't kick us out. I mean, see if we can work something out with the electric company. I suppose. I don't know."

Guy said: "At least we got the oven going, maybe eventually it will warm the whole place."

Buddy said: "Yeah, maybe."

Just then the gas started flickering. They could hear it in the oven. Little spits of air came out. The oven turned off. The percolator stopped percolating. Buddy tried all of the burners. None of them worked. Buddy sighed. He looked over at Guy and frowned.

Buddy said: "Shit, they shut the gas off."

Guy said: "Yeah, but who? Don't they have to do that by hand or something?"

Buddy said: "Oh, I don't know."

Guy said: "Look out the window, quick! Maybe the guy will take us to the gas station!"

Guy and Buddy ran to the back door. They could see a truck in the alley. A WyoGas logo on its side. Buddy opened the door. A gust of wind blew it open. Guy tried to run out. He didn't get very far. The truck drove away. Guy turned back around and came inside. His hair was spiked. At all angles. His big brown puppy dog eyes. Guy went into the living room and picked up their stocking caps from the last time they had tried to fight the wind. He handed Buddy his stocking cap. He put his own stocking cap on.

Buddy said: "Well, you win some, you lose some."

The End.

Thanks to:
George Truman
Jess Barbagallo
Tina Satter
Scott Halvorsen Gillette
Miette Gillette

About the Author

Joey Truman is a writer. He is the inventor of the Tickler, the Cubby Bubby, and Dykes on a Stick.

About the Publisher

Whisk(e)y Tit is committed to restoring degradation and degeneracy to the literary arts. We work with authors who are unwilling to sacrifice intellectual rigor, unrelenting playfulness, and visual beauty in our literary pursuits, often leading to texts that would otherwise be abandoned in today's largely homogenized literary landscape. In a world governed by idiocy, our commitment to these principles is an act of civil service and civil disobedience alike.

www.ingramcontent.com/pod-product-compliance
Lightning Source LLC
Chambersburg PA
CBHW050319120526
44592CB00014B/1967